THE ART OF COMMERCIAL MORTGAGE BROKERING

Evaldo Dupuy

The Art of Commercial Mortgage Brokering

Evaldo Dupuy

ISBN 09777789-0-8

Design and Production by Middle River Press L.L.C.

middleriverpress.com

Table of Contents

Chapter 4

Chapter 5

Chapter 6

Chapter 7

Chapter 8

Chapter 9

Chapter 10

Chapter 11

Chapter 12

Chapter 13

Chapter 20

Chapter 21

Chapter 22

Chapter 23

Section III: Form & Letter Templates for use in Commercial Mortgage Brokering

Introduction to the Art of Brokering

What is Brokering?

Definition of a Broker: A person or entity who, for a fee, acts as the agent of another, assisting in arranging a transaction. A broker acts as an agent for others in negotiating contracts, purchases, or sales of any financing or service without owning the financing or service. A broker does not take ownership for the financing or service.

In simpler terms, a broker takes someone who wants to buy and someone who wants to sell and introduces them. What happens from there depends upon the level of mutual attraction. A good broker knows what qualities both parties seek in a potential partner. A successful broker knows how to prepare an attractive loan package to help bring buyer and seller together. Both buyer and seller benefit when a good match is made, and the broker receives a fee for his or her services. The fee may come from the buyer, the seller, or both. Chances are, many things in your life were obtained through a broker. If the books on your shelf were purchased through Amazon.com, or you found your dentist through a referral service, you've used a broker's services. If you found your job through an employment agency or a car through an on-line service, you've gone through a broker.

The art of brokering is integral to the function of human society. Commercial mortgage brokering is an essential part of successful businesses, both large and small. This book is dedicated to brokering the individual and corporate-owned businesses that make up the heart of American society. Small commercial mortgages, ranging from $250,000 to $5 million, help create the many and varied individual franchises that line your city's streets. There is tremendous, untapped potential in the small commercial-mortgage market, which I want to share with you. My success as a commercial real estate mortgage broker is a result of the quality that I have consistently delivered in over thirty years of business. In this book, I share the secrets to my own success and provide you with the knowledge that you need to succeed as a broker.

The best part about brokering is that it offers anyone with a little knowledge and determination the opportunity to make a six-figure income. If you are a residential mortgage broker, a commercial real estate broker, or a real estate attorney who wants to provide financial services to your clients, then this book is for you. If you are a financial advisor, accountant, or anyone who provides financial services to small business, then this book is also for you. Being in the industry will give you the background knowledge to learn the art of commercial mortgage brokering quickly and easily. But you don't need to be in the real estate or finance industries to become a commercial mortgage broker. This book is also for the entrepreneur. The fact is that very few people in the real estate or finance business know the ins and outs of obtaining commercial real estate loan funding. That is why a commercial mortgage broker brings such value to each client's transaction. By learning the specialized knowledge provided in this book, you can offer substantial value to both lenders and borrowers, and receive wonderful compensation for your work.

If you have the interest and the desire to learn this artform, you too can be a commercial mortgage broker. Everything you need to know to become a successful commercial mortgage broker is contained in this book. The *Art of Commercial Mortgage Brokering* represents thirty years of passion, knowledge, and commitment to the art of brokering. My philosophy is that you should not only deliver what you promise—every time—but you should also go above and beyond your customers' expectations. Customer satisfaction is of the utmost importance, and by building a database of satisfied customers, you will generate more business for yourself in the long run.

Almost Everyone You Deal With Is a Broker

The best known brokerage businesses are real estate, mortgage, insurance, and stocks and bonds. Companies also broker hotel rooms (for example Hotels. com), sales leads, books (Amazon.com), art (Art.com), employment (Monster. com), businesses (Biz by Sell.com), trucks, boats, boat charters, used and new construction equipment, health club memberships, oil, cotton, gasoline, pig bellies, seminars, franchises, commercial loans, money, receivables, advertising space—the list is endless.

We cannot discuss brokering without mentioning E-Bay. In a few short years E-Bay has turned out to be one of the largest brokers in the world. Think about it. E-Bay does not own what it sells. It only provides a marketing platform for selling other people's goods and services. The principle is simple; if a financing or service exists, it can be brokered.

Did you know that a huge market exists for brokering clean air? Clean air? Yes, you can broker clean air. Take, for example, a manufacturing plant that pollutes the air by producing excess emissions. The law allows such a plant to purchase clean air from a viable seller, in this case a country with a tiny manufacturing base and plenty of trees. The polluter can pay the clean air country to use their clean air. If you know who to call to buy clean air and who to call to sell it, you can make some serious money. My point is that if it exists and the seller will pay you a commission, it can be brokered, and if it can be brokered, you just built a brokerage business.

Simple financing is the easiest to sell. Of course, the simpler the financing, the smaller your commission will be. For example, I own a 50-foot boat. For tax reasons, the boat is available for charter. In order to charter it, I have to market it. Since marketing such a small-market financing in such a vast world is not economically feasible, I enlisted with a yacht chartering company, a broker, who actively advertises and markets it. Whenever the boat is chartered, the broker receives 25% of the rental. This particular charter company has over 500 yachts in its fleet. It does not own any of them, but they have a web presence, advertise in boating magazines, and sponsor a booth at all major boat shows to promote their products and services. The owner of the brokerage company earns over $50,000 net a month in commissions. After he deducts his cost for marketing, his take home is in the $30,000 range. Not bad for renting someone else's boat.

Some of the largest companies in the world are brokers. Look at the stock brokerage industry: Merrill Lynch, Solomon Brothers, Schwab, and Ameritrade. They are all brokers. In the real estate market there is Century 21, Lending Tree, CB Richard Ellis, and hundreds of others. The insurance industry also operates with the use of brokers or agents. In the travel industry, all travel agents are brokers.

The Internet is full of brokers; every affiliate program is a brokerage because they promote someone else's products and get paid when a financing is sold. Every industry needs brokers. Brokering is now becoming a home-based business able to compete with the big boys. With the advent of laptop computers, cell phones, and other simple-to-use communication tools, a home-based brokerage business can offer you a wonderful opportunity for significant income. These days, all you need to be a broker is to determine the financing or service you want to sell, obtain a brokering or marketing agreement with your financing suppliers, and obtain a phone, a fax, and a computer. You're in business.

The *Art of Commercial Mortgage Brokering* teaches you how to structure a small-commercial-mortgage request to obtain the best possible financing for your clients. You will learn how to find potential clients and how to analyze a potential transaction for risk and profitability. This book and the companion CD, *CRES Solutions: Your Key to the Financing Vault*, provide you with all the information and business forms you need to prepare a preliminary underwriting. Additionally, I teach you how to select the appropriate institutional lender and how to make sure your package will appeal to that lender.

The best part about brokering is that you don't have to have a large bank account in order to succeed. All you need to know is your financing and how to sell it well, and this book will teach you exactly that.

How Do I Become a Broker?

The first sixteen chapters of this book provide you a significant amount of information regarding the different kinds of properties and commercial mortgages available. As you read them, you will learn how to spot a good deal, both from the buyer's perspective and the lender's. Over time, as you become familiar with the information provided in these chapters, you will be able to structure your own initial lending packages, and you will begin to develop direct relationships with lenders. While you are learning, I recommend you utilize the database of lenders provided at www.cresguide.com (CRES Guide is the acronym for Commercial Real Estate Services Guide). This is a database of lenders and investors with whom I have personally built relationships over the years. The professionals at *cresguide.com* can also help you by preparing loan packages that meet these lenders' requirements. You will still receive a fee for your services, even as you are learning the business.

While you study the information in this book, you can begin your own brokerage business by following these steps:

1. Check on your state's licensing requirements.

• ONLY CALIFORNIA, NEVADA, AND ARIZONA REQUIRE LICENSES. If you are in any other state, you can skip this step.

2. Choose an area of commercial real estate finance in which to specialize.

• Get to know those specific loan products well. (See Chapters 6, 7, and 9 for a complete discussion of your options.)

3. Find lenders.

• Go to *cresguide.com* and search for lenders that provide financing for your area of expertise.

• Or, if you already have lender contacts, approach them directly.

• Remember, the primary value a broker brings to a potential borrower is options. If you don't already have a stable of lenders, you can sign up with *cresguide.com* and take advantage of the lender relationships I have built. This fee-based service allows you to begin earning money as a broker right away. You can use all or some of the services provided at *cresguide.com*, including help with loan preparation.

4. Fill out an application with the lender(s) to become an authorized broker.

• On *cresguide.com*, you can look up the lender's policy for working with brokers and download the application to become an authorized broker (you need to be authorized by lenders who pay referral fees.) Fill it out and send it in.

5. Find & qualify potential clients.

• This involves marketing, which is overviewed in Chapter 1, and discussed in detail in Section II, Chapters 17–23.

• The companion CD contains software which allows you to quickly qualify a potential client. (See detailed discussion in Chapter 2 on Qualifying Leads.)

• Both the Appendix of this book and the companion CD contain marketing letter templates that you can use to attract clients.

6. Have your client sign a brokerage agreement.

• This ensures you are paid for your services.

• A copy of the agreement is found in the Appendix of this book.

7. Prepare and submit a first cut loan package to the lender.

• As a beginner in the commercial mortgage finance world, you can sign up with my professional staff at Coast Investors and have them package, present and process your loans for you. You will still receive a 0.5% to 1% brokers' fee on these transactions. Coast Investors, Inc, a company I own, (*www. coastinvestors.com*) is a wholesaler with existing relationships with several major lenders.

• OR—You can utilize the software on the companion CD to prepare your loan packages. The *CRES Solutions CD* contains all of the software you need to qualify a client and prepare a first cut. Simply input the information into the required fields and let the software calculate the numbers for you. It is recommended that you start out with Coast Investors while you are learning the ropes and learning to work with the software on the CD.

That's it. If you've done your job qualifying your potential borrower, the loan has an excellent chance of being funded. That is the key to the commercial mortgage brokerage industry—to work with applicants who have a high probability of getting funded. Your commission depends upon this, and upon making sure you have a signed brokerage agreement with your potential borrower.

Section I

YOUR KEY TO THE FINANCING VAULT

CHAPTER ONE

Developing Your Brokerage Business

The key to originating commercial mortgages is to have a good understanding of both the borrower's and the lender's needs.

Lender needs are always the same. The lender wants to lend money in a profitable way to someone who is a good risk. Thus, your ability to analyze the deal risk and present your analysis to the lender is crucial to your success. This book guides you step by step through the underwriting risk analysis process (called a "first cut") and even provides a detailed example of how to write up your analysis and present it successfully to the lender. The forms you need to prepare a first cut are provided and demonstrated in this book. In addition, they are available on the companion CD, entitled *CRES Solutions: Your Key to the Financing Vault*.

This book and the *CRES Solutions CD* provide you all the knowledge and tools you need to get started. New and experienced brokers can also benefit from the many services offered on our website, *www.cresguide.com*. If you can find a suitable borrower, the professionals at *cresguide.com* can help you find a suitable lender. We can also help you prepare a professional loan package to present to the lender, allowing you to concentrate on building your clientele while you learn to prepare the deals yourself.

Borrower needs vary. Each potential client has different needs, and your ability as a commercial mortgage broker to offer your borrowers a range of options gives both you and the borrower an advantage. But to suitably meet your borrower's needs, you absolutely must educate yourself about the various finance options available, as well as marketplace trends. Specialization allows you to manage this large body of information and to serve your clients' needs more specifically. Therefore, your first step in developing a successful small commercial mortgage business is to specialize in a particular sector of the market.

Within the small-commercial finance world, there are many possible areas of specialization. Small apartment buildings, trailer parks, marinas, hotels, motels, bed and breakfasts, gas stations, restaurants, small strip-shopping centers, and auto repair facilities are just a few examples of specialized market segments. Get in your car and drive one mile in either direction on any major commercial street. You will see countless small businesses housed in commercial buildings. Go to any warehouse district and you will find hundreds of small service, distribution or light manufacturing facilities that offer you business potential. Each one of these business entities is a potential client every five years. I say every five years, because unlike the residential real estate mortgage market, where loans are fixed for 30 years, the commercial real estate market typically issues a five-, seven- or ten-year mortgage, amortized over 20 years (30 years for multifamily properties). However, in recent years several investors like Coast Investors, GE Capital, La Salle Bank, and an old, well-known and well-funded Wall Street firm have been offering 25-year fixed commercial mortgages that become very attractive to borrowers in a climbing interest rate environment.

To be a successful broker, you should select one or two markets in which to specialize, and here is where you will target your marketing and advertising efforts. You might select small apartment complexes (under 60 units,) owner occupied properties, small shopping centers, or manufactured housing communities as your target markets.

Make a list of the markets that interest you. Once that is done, research the market to find out about the demand. Your next step is to find lenders that are willing to pay you commissions or a referral fee for brokering loans to them. I have spent 35 years building relations with lenders. This book gives you the tools and information you need to do this yourself. Additionally, you can opt to take advantage of my experience by utilizing the database of lenders on *cresguide.com*. In most small-commercial transactions, the lender allows the broker to receive a brokerage fee and also receive a yield spread fee; the lender will require you to have a signed agreement with the borrower for your brokerage fee.

You must have a brokering agreement that spells out what you will do to sell someone else's financing and how much compensation you will receive. GET IT IN WRITING. I once lost a $250,000 commission because the seller was in a hurry to sell, I had a buyer at hand, I set up the deal without having the contract signed in order to expedite matters for the seller, and in the long run he did not pay my commission. I had no recourse because I did not have a signed document. I cannot emphasize it enough. If it's not in writing, forget it! A copy of such an agreement is printed in Section III of this book, and a customizable form is available on the *CRES Solutions* CD. Some lenders will pay you yield spread in addition to your brokerage fee. At this point I like to introduce the concept of getting paid in the front (a brokerage fee from the borrower) and in the back (a referral fee from the lender). Yes, you read it right, in small-commercial brokerage you can get paid by the borrower and the investor, and it is legal.

Most commercial mortgages end up in a Wall Street securitization. Many mortgage companies and banks say they make commercial mortgages, when, in fact, they are only originating the mortgage for resale to Wall Street conduits or investment banks. These conduits and banks then package and sell the mortgages into securitizations. The more people between you, the broker, and the Wall Street securitization process, the more expensive you have to make your mortgage package in order to profit. Accordingly, originating and funding commercial mortgages requires a significant knowledge of the commercial mortgage business, as well as knowledge of the securitization structures that ultimately provide the liquid capital. This book provides you with comprehensive knowledge of commercial mortgage business fundamentals, from marketing and originating commercial mortgages, to Wall Street securitization markets, where all mortgages eventually wind up.

To be a successful broker, your knowledge of the borrower's wants, needs, requirements, and desires should be paired with knowledge of the commercial mortgage process. The knowledge of this process, from underwriting and risk analysis to creation of a proper loan package, is the very backbone of a profitable commercial mortgage business.

When looking for a commercial mortgage, a borrower's first inclination is to contact his local banker friend—the same guy who financed his house or with whom he plays golf on the weekends. Most borrowers do not realize that banks are not the best option for a commercial mortgage. Usually, the local bank is only interested in making a commercial loan if the borrower has a significant amount of money on deposit with the bank or if the bank can also get a second mortgage on the house, the wife and the kids! Although banks are rarely interested in making commercial loans, they are still a terrific source of referrals. Often the bank is kind enough to refer the loan to a commercial mortgage broker or lender that can better serve the borrower. Institutional (nonbank) investors, like Coast Investors, can offer more attractive financing packages than banks, and often at a more competitive rate. Thus, a bank offers limited options for commercial mortgages, but an institutional investor can offer more options to the borrower. Coast Investors, for example, specializes in stated income/stated asset loans up to $1,000,000. A good commercial real estate mortgage broker researches the market on behalf of his or her client to obtain more attractive and more suitable financing (e.g., long-term, fixed-rate financing) at a more competitive rate. The key to originating commercial mortgage business is to understand the value you bring to the transaction. Most borrowers do not even know that commercial mortgage specialists exist, so it is up to you to educate your clients on the benefits you can offer them.

The number one benefit from the perspective of many of your clients is a low interest rate. Whether you solicit the property owner directly, or through an intermediary such as a commercial realtor or a financial advisor, they will all tell you the same thing: that he or she is looking for the lowest possible interest rate.

There are several key elements to understand before you can determine if "rate" is the primary factor for a borrower. The key elements include, but are not limited to:

The loan term and amortization schedule. The loan term lets the borrower know when he/she will have to refinance, and the amortization schedule influences the monthly payment. A longer amortization means a smaller monthly payment.

Fixed or variable rate. During periods of rising interest rates, like the present time, borrowers should demand—and you should offer—fixed rates for at least 5 years. During periods of declining interest rates you should offer a variable rate loan and explain to your client that a fixed rate will lock them into a less desirable rate.

Full documentation vs. stated income stated asset. Stated income loans are relatively new to the commercial finance world and are limited to about

$1,000,000. Stated loans are usually faster to close than full documentation loans because your client will not need to deliver as much tax documentation to obtain the loan. Thus, from a client's perspective, they offer the benefit of simplicity. Lenders who offer stated loans for multifamily up to $5,000,000 include institutional lenders, like Coast Investors, as well as large multifamily lenders.

Your borrower's tolerance for prepayment penalty, lockout or yield maintenance. This question is usually directly related to how long a borrower expects to own a property. If a borrower intends to hold a property for at least 10 years, he should not object to a 5 year, 5% prepayment penalty.

Willingness to pay upfront fees and closing fees (e.g., underwriting, appraisal, engineering, environmental, etc.). Is this borrower really serious about a loan, and if so, does he have the money to pay for the expenses of origination a loan? Appraisal, environmental, and application fees can run $15,000. Additionally, to close the loan you have closing and legal fees, as well as loan and brokerage fees.

Recourse or nonrecourse options. A recourse option gives lenders the right to come after the rest of borrower's assets in case of default on the primary loan. When a borrower wants a nonrecourse deal, he should expect a lower LTV and a higher interest rate. Banks typically do not offer non recourse oans; they are usually found in conduit financings.

Cross-default, cross-collateralization, ability to obtain release provisions, ability to obtain lease provisions. (Does the borrower need the ability to obtain lease provisions?)

After investigating, you may find the borrower would be best suited for a REIT transaction, a conduit-type transaction or a private lender transaction, as compared to a local bank transaction. The ability to advise the borrower, and offer several financing options, creates significant value to the borrower.

Another important contributor to adding value to a transaction is knowledge of the underwriting process and risk analysis. Often, the appearance of the deal at the time of submission differs from the end result of the final term sheet. This is because cash flows vary for every commercial property, and unless the broker understands the issues and demonstrates the underwriting risk in the loan package, the lender will have difficulty providing an "accurate" quote. This book provides a detailed sample of a commercial property write-up; a write-up analyzes the property, the market, the financials, and the borrower, and is presented to the investor in a simplified format, five to seven pages long, so that he does not have to spend a lot of time going through hundreds of pages in order to find the information. Always provide the investor with all of the important facts up front, particularly the negative aspects of the transaction. If you do this consistently, the investor will always look at the deals you present. If you misrepresent a fact to a lender or try to hide information, the lender will put you on virtual black list and you will not get any deals done with the lender. Your relationship with the lenders is what keeps you in business. Deals come and go but lenders and investors who are willing to pay referral fees are hard to find and have to be protected.

For example, for a lender to provide an accurate quote on a retail property, the lender will often reconstruct the operating statement in order to calculate the gross income and subtract a vacancy reserve, normalize the income and expenses, and then adjust the expenses using an expense growth rate. Then property-specific underwriting parameters are applied in order to calculate the stabilized Net Cash Flow (NCF), direct capitalized value, to Value (LTV), and Debt (DSCR). This is what I have previously referred to as a "first cut." A successful broker will complete the first cut for the lender prior to submitting a loan package. Providing a solid first cut to a lender paves the way for them to accept the deal. So the keys to originating commercial mortgages include understanding the borrower's deal points and analyzing the underwriting risk of the transaction (completing a first cut.) A strong understanding of these issues, properly communicated to the lender, gives you the ability to negotiate the best terms and rate on behalf of your client.

Successful Brokers Are Great Marketers

Developing a successful marketing strategy is an essential part of your brokering success. Your main assets are your investors, your clients and your ability to generate new clients. This involves marketing.

Commercial mortgage brokerage is a service. Your job is to find companies or individuals who wish to purchase or refinance their commercial real estate property. Then you must find an appropriate institutional commercial or private lender, and place the two parties together. Only work with purchasers who are willing to pay you a commission for finding them the financing they need. Foremost, you need a stable of funding sources whose loan programs you know well. In the *CRES Solutions* CD, you will find a list of major institutional lenders that can fund your loan package.

To develop a successful brokerage business you have to create and implement a strategic marketing plan that includes all of the following components:

- Your marketing strategy should be tailored to provide you with a significant commercial mortgage brokerage presence, to include a website specifically designed to sell your services.

- A powerful direct marketing "snail mail" advertising campaign consisting of postcards and correspondence aimed at potential buyers.

- Print ads in general and trade publications read by potential clients.

- A public relations and press release program designed to get your name and your company's name in trade publications and regular consumer papers and magazines.

- For some brokers, a seminar series is also a great marketing tool.

- Above all, develop and implement a great service. After all, service is what you provide. A reputation for providing great service is your most valuable marketing tool.

- Each one of these steps plays an important role in your overall strategy and must be developed to its fullest potential. If even one step fails, your chances of success will be significantly reduced.

Section II of this book describes the marketing and selling techniques that I have used successfully over the years. Traditional techniques for marketing include active marketing, such as cold calling, and passive marketing, such as advertising. The most effective approach is active marketing that involves a combination of direct mail (cover letter with sample loan package) and a follow-up phone call. Whether the first call results in business or not, it is recommended that every new client is added to your monthly newsletter mailing.

In Section III of this book, and on the *CRES Solutions* CD, you will find sample letters to send to a property owner, real estate broker, or financial advisor, as well as a sample advertisement.

When you call to follow up with a prospective client, you should reiterate the opening paragraph of the appropriate sample letter. We suggest that you study all of the training materials provided in this book prior to making these calls. Once you make the call, you may be required to discuss a deal—and the best way to discuss a deal is by asking the right questions BEFORE agreeing to work on a loan.

CHAPTER TWO

Let's Start With the Basics

Deal Flow: The Heart of a Brokering Money Machine.

Section II of the book deals with marketing to obtain deals from multiple sources. This chapter gives you an overview of who your clients should be—in other words, who you should market to—in order to obtain a consistent deal flow.

Finding sources for leads can be a relatively simple but time-consuming task. While there are many online websites and list brokers offering information about commercial property owners, commercial real estate brokers, and financial advisors, it is recommended you focus your efforts locally, which gives you the ability to meet potential clients in person. Borrowers and lead sources often prefer to interact with other local professionals. Furthermore, finding these sources in your local area is relatively inexpensive—you only need to search the yellow pages, business directories, or spend a day at the local county assessor's office examining property ownership records.

Commercial Property Owners

Commercial property owners make great clients for several reasons. Many commercial real estate loans are not fully amortizing and have loans that may be due in one to five years. Although there are 10- and 15-year terms available for most commercial properties, many commercial properties are financed by local banks that choose to make only short-term variable rate loans, partly due to restrictions imposed by the banking regulators (e.g., OCC, OTS, FDIC, etc.). As such, there is always a market for commercial real estate financing, regardless of interest rate fluctuations and the economy.

It is recommended that you contact every title company in your area for commercial property leads. The quality of leads they can provide may vary, but this is the simplest and least expensive source for identifying when a property owner's loan is due. We suggest you request loans that have nine months or less left until the loan is due.

The direct source for identifying property owners in your county is the county assessor's office or recorder of deeds. Here you will find information on every property in the county, contact information, date of last sale, sale price, etc. This information is typically available for free (as it is public record), though you are encouraged to call ahead to determine whether there are charges for copies of the information.

Virtually every property owner has an opinion of the value of his property holdings, whether based upon personal opinion or an appraisal. Property owners spend a great deal of time and money seeking attractive financing, but often waste money on fees because they have received an inaccurate quote from an unqualified mortgage broker. Your ability to properly analyze their property value and the underwriting risks associated with the deal protects the borrower from receiving inaccurate information and protects you from soliciting the wrong type of financing based on the borrower's inaccurate information.

An excellent technique for marketing to property owners is to hold seminars where you illustrate the process by which their property will be analyzed from a lender's perspective. Show them how a comprehensive "first cut" underwriting addresses the key deal points needed to successfully solicit lenders. This approach puts you, the broker, in a better position to accurately represent the borrower's financing requirements and subsequently obtain the best and most accurate quote.

Commercial Real Estate Brokers

The benefit of marketing to real estate brokers is that brokers have multiple deals in process at all times. A creative mailer, emphasizing your ability to finance the more difficult deal—such as when the buyer/borrower wants to finance on a stated basis—can result in relationships that will give you a significant amount of business. The best source for finding commercial real estate brokers in your area is your local yellow pages. Consider marketing to the individual real estate broker or agent or to the senior broker at that office. Consider sponsoring and speaking at a seminar for brokers advising them how to effectively gather information that will make for a smooth loan process.

It is important to note that real estate brokers commonly focus on upside potential when presenting a commercial property. As you may have learned by now, commercial real estate finance is not about upside, it is about present value. When you discuss property values, there are two realities at play—the real estate broker's reality, which is based on what he thinks he can get for the property, and the mortgage broker's reality, which is based on how much he thinks a lender will fund. Both realities are correct. For example, a real estate broker lists a property for $5,000,000, but the value of the "cash flows" is only $4,500,000. If the real estate broker finds someone willing to buy it for $5,000,000, the lender will likely only lend up to 80 percent of $4,500,000 (the direct capitalized value) and the buyer will have to come up with a larger down payment.

By offering to qualify a broker's listings for financing, you are helping the broker manage a potential buyer's expectations and providing new tools for the broker to market the property to prospective buyers.

Most real estate brokers recognize they cannot complete a sale unless the prospective purchaser can obtain suitable financing. You bring value to a real estate transaction in several ways. Your first cut underwriting can validate a listing price or further support the strength of a purchase offer. Just because a property is listed at $5,000,000, does not mean it is worth $5,000,000.

An effective technique used in marketing to realtors is to illustrate (in underwriting terms) the financial issues with a property's cash flows and how those issues will require certain underwriting parameters (e.g., vacancy reserves, TI/LCs, income trends, etc.). This provides the realtor with additional insight to establish the right listing price, identify the right buyer, manage the financing expectations, and, essentially, have a prepackaged loan request ready for the buyer. It is recommended that you offer this type of prepackaging for every new listing the realtor takes. On the *CRES Solutions* CD, you will find a package for each property type that you can give a real estate broker to help him with this work.

Financial Advisors

Financial advisors, by definition, have the relationships with property owners that can help the broker get into the largest and sweetest deals. While financial advisors advise their clients on financial matters, few are educated in the art of underwriting small commercial mortgage loans. By providing commercial mortgage advice to these professionals, you can gain their referral business. The information you offer helps them better advise their clients who own investment properties. You will also find that bankers who do not have the ability to provide commercial mortgage loans (especially stated commercial loans) would rather provide a referral source than turn away a current or prospective depositor empty-handed.

An effective technique for marketing to financial advisors is to educate them about the issues that can affect the underwriting of their clients' commercial properties. The best way I have found is to hold paid or free seminars on the subject. During the seminar, emphasize how you are available to discuss clients' commercial properties financing needs prior to taking a referral.

If you decide to provide stated income/stated asset commercial loans, make sure you market these products to CPAs, financial planners, real estate attorneys, estate planners, and local banks. Often, a personal referral by a trusted financial professional can be very valuable.

Now that you know who your potential clients are, I'd like to share a word about the environment in which you will be working, the real estate market.

Real Estate Markets

Real estate is a cyclical industry that is affected by both local and national economic conditions, including growth in population and employment, consumer spending, interest rates, and inflation. While macroeconomic conditions are important factors affecting the overall state of the real estate industry, local supply and demand conditions are by far the most important factors that affect real estate markets.

The five primary real estate sectors are office, retail, industrial, hospitality, and residential (multifamily and 1- to 4-family). A lender's commercial real estate and construction lending may be targeted to one or more of these five primary real estate sectors. Each market sector has its own characteristics. In the office sector, the demand for office space is highly dependent on white collar employment. Office space expansion generally lags behind economic recoveries. In the retail sector, rental rates and the demand for retail space are affected by employment rates, as well as by consumer confidence and spending. The industrial sector is influenced by consumer spending levels, inventory levels, defense spending, and the volume of national exports. The hospitality sector is affected by the strength of the U.S. dollar; a weak dollar induces foreign visitors to travel to the United States, while prompting Americans to vacation in the States. The hospitality sector of the real estate market is additionally motivated by consumer spending, the price of air travel, and business conditions. Finally, in the multifamily residential sector, the demand for apartments is heavily influenced by the affordability of ownership housing, local employment conditions, and the vacancy of existing inventory.

Population growth is a key factor for all sectors of the real estate industry because it influences consumer spending and the demand for goods and services. It also influences federal appropriations and state funding for local infrastructure projects and other services directly affecting real estate markets. Changing demographics, such as increases in the level of immigrants or retirees, are also important factors affecting real estate markets.

Qualifying a Lead

Not all leads you receive are worth working on, and it's important to be able to quickly qualify a loan during the first conversation with your client. Since the income of the property determines the value of the property as well as the financing risk, you can quickly qualify a commercial mortgage loan request by asking for a few simple pieces of information:

What type of property is it? Apartment, retail, warehouse, hotel, office, trailer park, etc.

Property's Net Operating Income (NOI) for the most current full year. Also get the NOI year-to-date. The NOI will be discussed in greater detail later in Chapter 3. Put simply, it is income minus operating expenses. The figures should include debt service (mortgage payments) and depreciation or amortization. Do not include income and expenses that are attributable to the borrower's business or personal expenses.

Purchase price if a purchase or estimated value if a refinance.

Divide the NOI by the capitalization rate (cap rate) to obtain the approximate market value of the property in question.

(A detailed discussion of cap rates appears in Chapter 3.) As a general rule of thumb, use a 9% cap rate for most property types. Use 7.5% for multifamily and 12% for hotel. During the hot real estate market of the 2000s, cap rates have declined as purchase prices have gone up. In California, cap rates for apartment buildings have gone to as low as 5.1.

For newer construction, take the projected NOI divided by the capitalization rate as above.

Most investors, especially those making small commercial loans up to $5,000,000, require that you provide them with a tri-merge credit report with credit scores. The *CRES Solutions* CD provides you with a list of companies that offer tri merge credit reports. A credit score of less than 660 will not get the deal done; or, if the borrower is lucky, he may be offered a loan at interest rates that are 1 to 2 percentage points higher than a prime mortgage loan.

While the above purchase price calculation is a quick, cursory method, it will provide you with some basis to determine the quality of the lead. For more accurate results, use the software provided in the *CRES Solutions* CD to calculate NOI. You can input the data directly into the form provided on the CD as you receive it from the potential client. Rather than just collecting NOI for each year, you will need to ask for and input income and expense figures and also input one entry into the rent roll. Then let the software calculate NOI in order to get an underwriting. Practice a few times with fictitious data before you try this while a client is on the phone.

If the value of the property is in line with what your client believes the property is worth, then it's time to move to the next step. Write it up and send it to your lender/investor.

If you do not have a lender, or if you lack the time or knowledge to prepare the credit write up, *you can also send it to us at Coast Investors and let us do the work for you.* You will still receive a fee, ranging from 0.5% to 1%, as calculated on the loan amount.

What the Investor Needs to Know.

For a lender/investor to start processing a loan application, he must have:

• A lender's application;

• The current rent roll, this to include each tenant's contract rent, lease start date, lease end date, leased area, and what expenses are paid by the tenant (reimbursements);

• Property tax returns or operating statements for one to three years.

If the value of the property IS NOT in line with what your client believes the property is worth, then seek to determine if you may be missing information that would support a higher valuation. In this scenario, manage the borrower's expectations as to why there is a difference, or simply walk away from this particular deal. Unrealistic or unmanageable clients can be a waste of time.

Other Qualifying Factors

In addition to the primary information, other factors influence the determination of financing risk, and each property type has its own qualifying factors. Some additional factors are:

• Market: Established or developing market with a minimum population of 50,000 is preferred, with no quantifiable population declines since 1980, based on US Census data.

• Property: Post-1980 construction is preferred.

• Operating Performance: The property will show strong operating performance with no material declines in revenue or net operating income over the past two years.

You can verify some of this data by checking local market sources. Good online sources for local market data can be found on the following websites:

http://www.BlacksGuide.com www.loopnet.com http://www.Apartment-Seeker.com

At any of these websites, you can search for other properties in the state and county where your property is located in order to help you estimate market rent, market vacancy, and other valuable market data.

Quoting an Interest Rate

Before a lender or investor can quote you a rate, he needs to understand the financing risk of the property, and that means calculating the stabilized net cash flow using the past one to three years of income and expenses, normalized, adjusted for inflation, and with the appropriate underwriting reserves applied. In other words, it is unreasonable to request a rate quote without first determining the LTV, Debt Service Coverage Ratio (DSCR), and the overall loan risk. (See Chapter 3 for a detailed breakdown of these numbers.) While some lenders post rates, the posted rate simply represents the best rate available for the least amount of risk. Therefore, you can soft quote the "best available rate" to your prospective client, but qualify your quote by stating that you will need to understand the financing risk of the property to quote a more reliable interest rate.

CHAPTER THREE

The Numbers and What They Mean

Introduction to Financial Analysis

Commercial financing for commercial real estate properties is underwritten on a case-by-case basis. Every loan application is unique and evaluated on its own merits, but there are a few common criteria lenders look for in commercial loan packages. This chapter breaks down the most important numbers used in analyzing potential loans. But first, let's look at a quick overview of the critical factors that most every lender uses when analyzing a potential loan.

The "processing" of a loan is an attempt to verify the numbers associated with the purchase or refinancing of a property. The processing and due-diligence should prove that the buyer or owner will not be overburdened by debt as a result of buying or refinancing the property. This is accomplished by analyzing both the property and the buyer.

Commercial Mortgage Lending Ratios

Some aspects of the analysis can be converted into ratios, and these ratios are fairly effective indicators of a buyer's ability to handle the transaction.

Loan To Value Ratio (LTV)

The Loan to Value Ratio (LTV) is defined as follows:

Loan to Value = total loan balances (1st mortgage + 2nd mortgage) ÷ fair market value (as determined by a third party appraisal.)

For commercial mortgages, Loan to Value Ratios seldom exceed 75%, meaning no more than 75% of the fair market value will be funded by the lender. This can sometimes leave the buyer short, requiring the buyer to put down a larger down payment. Coast Investors and other specialty lenders lend up to 90% on owner-occupied real estate. (See Chapter 7 for a detailed discussion of owner-occupied real estate.)

Debt Service Coverage Ratio (DSCR)

Debt Service Coverage Ratio (DSCR) evaluates the ratio of property income to property debt. The Debt Service Coverage Ratio is defined as:

Debt Service Coverage Ratio = net operating income ÷ debt service

Debt service is the mortgage payment on the property. Most lenders insist that the DSCR ratio exceed 1.15. A debt service coverage ratio of less than 1.0 would mean that the property did not produce enough net rental income for the owner to make the mortgage payments without supplementing the property from his personal budget.

Personal Debt Service Coverage Ratio

Some lenders of small commercial loans (less than $1,000,000) also look at the personal income and debt of the borrowers.

The personal debt ratio compares the dollar amount of the bills that a borrower must pay each month to the amount of monthly income he earns from all sources. More precisely, the personal debt coverage ratio is defined as:

Personal Debt Coverage Ratio = monthly personal debt ÷ monthly personal income.

A personal debt ratio of 150% would mean that a borrower's obligations are one and a half times his income. Obviously, someone whose personal debt coverage ratio is 150% is in trouble. Personal debt ratios seldom are allowed to exceed 50% in practice.

Other Important Calculations

Net Operating Income (NOI)

Net Operating Income is the income from a rental property after deducting for real estate taxes, fire and liability insurance, maintenance, and all other operating expenses.

Capitalization Rate (Cap Rate)

The capitalization rate, or cap rate, is a ratio used to estimate the value of income producing properties. In general, the lower the cap rate, the higher the selling price of the property will be.

Additional Financial Factors to Analyze

Credit Worthiness

In many cases the personal credit of principals will be evaluated. Corporations are additionally evaluated for business performance and credit rating.

Property Analysis

A property's fair market value will be analyzed. Fair market value is determined by the appraisal and by fair market rents (the average rent paid in your market for properties similar to yours). Age, appearance, local market, location, and accessibility are some other factors to consider when analyzing the property. Special use properties may require additional underwriting.

Appraisers use the income approach, cost replacement, and market comparison methods to estimate the value of property (see Chapter 5). The income approach utilizes the theory of capitalization based on the value of the income.

Tenant Analysis

A thorough analysis of the current tenant(s) will be conducted. Lenders will evaluate the financial strength of the tenant, the number of years remaining on the current lease, and other relevant information regarding the tenant.

Breaking Down the Numbers

Now that we've overviewed the major factors lenders look for in a loan write-up, we are going to take a more detailed look at how you should obtain, calculate, and interpret the four most critical numbers: the NOI, the DSCR, the LTV, and the Cap Rate.

Net Operating Income

We will discuss Net Operating Income first because this number plays an important part from the very beginning of the loan process. Net Operating Income, or NOI, is determined by subtracting vacancies and operating expenses from a property's gross income.

Operating expenses include the following items: advertising, insurance, maintenance, property taxes, property management, repairs, supplies, utilities, etc. The more information you include, the more accurate your calculation will be. The *CRES Solutions* CD offers you easy-to-use software that lists all of the information you will need to obtain from your prospective client in order to calculate the NOI. With a little practice, you can learn to input this information right into the software to help you qualify your prospective client during the initial telephone contact.

While more information is better when figuring the NOI, be sure not to include anything that is not an operating expense. Operating expenses do not include improvements such as a new roof, personal property like a lawn mower, mortgage payments, income taxes, capital gains taxes, or loan origination fees.

Debt Service Coverage Ratio

A key component in making an underwriting evaluation of a commercial property is the debt service coverage ratio.

The **DSCR** is defined as the yearly debt payment compared to the adjusted gross income of the property in question, or:

Debt Service Coverage Ratio = Net Operating Income ÷ Debt Service

By using a DSCR of 1:1.15, a lender is saying that they are looking for a $1.15 in net income for each $1.00 mortgage payment. Typically a lender will determine the DSCR ratio based on annual figures, the yearly mortgage payment compared to the yearly net borrower income. The higher the DSCR ratio is, the more conservative the lender will be. Most lenders will never go below a 1:1 ratio (a dollar of debt payment per dollar of income available). At a 1:1 ratio, a property is breaking even. Anything less then a 1:1 ratio means the potential borrower is in a negative cash flow situation, thus raising the risk for the lender.

DSCRs are set by property type and what a lender perceives the risk to be. Today, apartment properties are considered to be the least risky category of investment lending. As such, lenders are more inclined to use smaller DSCRs when evaluating a loan request. Your Coast Investors loan officer can assist you with understanding the DSCR policies of each of the loan programs we offer.

Loan to Value

Unlike residential lending, commercial investment properties are viewed more conservatively. Many lenders will require a minimum of 35% of the purchase price to be paid by the buyer. However, some lenders will loan up to 90% of the purchase price to buyers based upon a buyer's credit worthiness and property analysis. The percentage of the purchase price that the lender is willing to loan is called the loan to value (LTV) percentage.

> *Loan to Value (LTV)* is the calculation of the loan amount divided by purchase price, expressed in a percentage format.
>
> *Loan Amount ÷ Purchase Price = LTV %*
>
> For example if you are buying an apartment building for $1,000,000 (purchase price) and want to borrow $800,000 (loan amount), you are asking for a loan of 80%.

Each lender is different and decides their LTV based upon the lender's enthusiasm for the project, the quality of the buyer, and the property. If you know what a lender's LTV requirements are, you can also calculate the loan amount by multiplying the purchase price by the LTV percentage. Keep in mind that the purchase price must also be supported by an appraisal. In the event that the appraisal shows a value less then the purchase price, the lender will use the lower of the two numbers to determine the LTV.

Capitalization Rate - (Cap Rate)

The capitalization rate, or cap rate, is a ratio used to estimate the value of income-producing properties. This section discusses how cap rates are calculated, how you can obtain an accurate, current cap rate, and how you will use the cap rate in your brokerage business.

The **cap rate** is the net operating income (NOI) of a
commercial property, divided by the sales price or value
of the property, and expressed as a percentage.

NOI ÷ Purchase Price = Cap Rate %

Investors, lenders and appraisers use the cap rate to estimate the purchase price
for different types of income-producing properties. So if you have the cap rate
and the net operating income of a property, you can determine the property's
true value, or purchase price.

NOI ÷ Cap Rate % = Purchase Price

A market cap rate is determined by evaluating the financial data of similar
properties that have recently sold in a specific market. It provides a more
reliable estimate of value than a market gross rent multiplier (GRM), since the
cap rate calculation utilizes more of a property's financial detail. The GRM
calculation only considers a property's selling price and gross rents. The cap
rate calculation incorporates a property's selling price, gross rents, nonrental
income, vacancy amount, and operating expenses. Thus the cap rate provides
the most reliable estimate of value.

When dealing with a seller and an interested buyer for a particular piece of
income property, the seller is trying to get the highest price for the property.
The lower the cap rate, the higher the price a seller will command. Thus the
buyer hopes for a higher cap rate to keep the selling price low. Investors and
lenders, as well as buyers, look for high cap rates. Remember, the lower the
selling price, the higher the cap rate. The higher the selling price, the lower the
cap rate. In summary, investors, lenders, and buyers prefer a higher cap rate.

The cap rate varies in different areas of the country and even in different areas
of a city for many reasons, such as desirability of location, level of crime, and
general condition of an area. You would expect lower capitalization rates in
newer or more desirable areas of a city and higher cap rates to compensate for
the added risk in less desirable areas. In a real estate market where net operating
incomes are increasing and cap rates are declining over time for a given type
of investment property, such as office buildings, property values are generally
on the rise. If net operating incomes are decreasing and capitalization rates are
increasing over time in a given market place, property values are declining.
During periods of increasing interest rates, the cap rates rise along with the

interest rates. This cap rate increase results from a drop in property prices associated with the higher cost of money. During periods of decreasing interest rates, such as the one experienced from the year 2000 to 2005, the cap rates decrease as interest rates come down. The net result is that property prices decrease, and properties become more affordable.

The general rule of thumb I've given you in the "Qualifying a Lead" section, earlier in this book, is to use a 9% cap rate for most property types, 7.5% for multifamily, and 12% for hotel. Given this general rule of thumb, a 7.0% market cap rate for multifamily properties would be considered low, whereas a 13% cap rate for hotel properties in your area would be considered high. You can compare the actual market cap rate against the general rule of thumb rates when discussing rough estimates with your prospective borrowers.

If you would like to find out what the cap rate is for a particular type of property in a given market place, check with an appraiser or lender in that area. Or go to one of the websites presented in the Introduction of this book and search for properties in your area. Be aware that the frequency of sales for commercial income properties in a given market place may be low; if so, reliable capitalization rate data may not be available. If you are able to obtain a market cap rate from an appraiser or lender for the type of property you are evaluating, check to see if the cap rate value was determined with recent sales of comparable properties or if it was constructed. When adequate financial data is unavailable, appraisers may construct a cap rate through analysis of its component parts, thus reducing the credibility of the results. Cap rates determined by evaluating the recent actions of buyers and sellers in a particular marketplace will produce the best market value estimate for a property.

If you are able to obtain a market cap rate, you can use this information to estimate what similar income properties should sell for. This will help you to gauge whether or not the asking price for a particular piece of property is high or low. Remember:

Cap Rate = NOI / Value

And:

Estimated Value = NOI / Cap Rate

If a property has an NOI of $120,000 and you have determined that cap rates in the area for this type of property average 12%, then the formula is: Market Value = 120,000 / 12%.

This gives you an estimated market value of $1,000,000. Remember, as the cap rate goes down, selling prices go up; therefore this same formula, calculated with a smaller cap rate of 6%, raises the price to $2,000,000. Conversely, a higher cap rate of 15% would give you an estimated property value of $800,000. You can see the importance of this number to your clients, as well as to the lenders you will work with.

This concludes our discussion of the critical numbers and most important factors that lenders review prior to approving a loan. Based on what you've just learned, which of the following prospective clients is more likely to get a loan?

CLIENT A wishes to purchase a multifamily rental building with 45 units. The market cap rate for similar properties is 7.3%. The property's DSCR is 1:1.05, and the borrower's personal debt service coverage ratio is 70%. The asking price of the property is $1,200,000, and the borrower wishes to finance 95% of this amount.

CLIENT B also wishes to purchase a multifamily rental building with 45 units. This property is in a different area of town, where the market cap rate is 7.8%. The property's DSCR is 1:1.25, and the borrower's personal debt service coverage ratio is 25%. The fair market value of the property is $1,000,000, and the borrower wishes to finance 75% of this amount.

If you chose Client B as the best bet, you've been paying attention! Take a moment and consider how you would manage Client A's expectations by explaining the numbers to him.

CHAPTER FOUR

Types of Loans and Lenders

Multifamily lenders range from specialty lenders, who offer multifamily loans as small as $100,000 on a stated basis, to Mae and Freddie Mac mortgage lenders, who offer low interest rate loans in transactions as large as $300,000,000.

Some established players offer small-deal financing options with Loan-to-Value (LTV) ratios of 80% or more and with fixed-rate debt in the 6%-to-7% range.

Unfortunately, many entrepreneurs aren't fully aware of the increasing availability of small loans from the bigger banks, conduit lenders or agencies that have traditionally targeted larger loans. That means that some investors are likely to be paying higher rates and accepting more onerous terms than necessary.

There are several high-volume lenders who have, in recent years, begun to emphasize their small-loan apartment programs. These lenders include major financial institutions such as Washington Mutual and LaSalle Bank, many Fannie Mae and Freddie Mac mortgage lenders (such as ARCS), large multifamily lender REITS, and some major Wall Street conduit lenders like Column Financial. Some of these major lenders offer nonrecourse, 80% LTV apartment mortgages as small as $500,000—an offering that was once reserved for the largest, most experienced multifamily investors.

However, the best loan for a given deal should reflect the borrower's financial goals. You should take your client's goal into account when discussing term length; leverage level; interest rate and structure; recourse considerations; speed and certainty of execution; reserve requirements; and any other pertinent factors. For example, borrowers who expect to hold properties for the longer term should take advantage of the low-rate environment and lock in fixed-rate deals at high leverage levels from lenders.

Smaller Loans, Older Properties

Most of the program's borrowers have older Class B and (especially) Class C apartments they're refinancing or buying and expect to hold for many years. Most opt for fixed-rate, nonrecourse loans with 10-year terms, but five-year deals are also available. LTV ratios range up to 80%.

Apartment investors with shorter-term plans should seek three- to five-year portfolio lenders such banks or REITs. These lenders offer more prepayment flexibility and require personal recourse. Many small-property investors tend to trade regularly and hence aim to avoid prepayment restrictions.

Commercial (Credit Based Loans)

Loans secured by real estate can be divided into two categories based on the source of repayment: credit-based loans and project financing. Credit-based loans are loans that are secured by real estate, but will be repaid from the borrower's business operations or personal assets. Although the primary collateral for the loan is real estate, the real estate is not the source of repayment. In many instances, these loans are used to finance the acquisition of an owner-occupied business property that has an economic life similar to the term of the loan. They can also be term loans used for other business purposes, such as working capital. In either case, repayment is expected from the cash flow of the business rather than from the underlying real estate.

Construction Loans (Project Financing)

The key to construction lending is the analysis of project financing. This analysis is extremely complex. Although project financing still relies on cash flow, the cash flow originates from the underlying real estate collateral, not from the expected cash flow of the developed property. Project financing is repayable primarily from income currently being produced (or anticipated) from existing or future improvements to real estate. Secondary sources of repayment for such a loan originate from the credit capacity of the borrower and any guarantees made by the borrower.

The borrower in project financing can choose to hold title to the real estate under any of the following legal entities: corporations, joint ventures, real estate investment trusts (REITs), or partnerships where the general partner is a subchapter S corporation. Borrowers have additional choices as to the legal entity they form to hold the real estate title, but those I have just listed are the most popular because they allow investors to maximize tax benefits while limiting personal liability.

Project financing transactions progress in phases based on the value added by the development of a parcel of real estate. Property must first be acquired; then it must be cleared and improved with sewers, utilities, and streets. Only then can a building be constructed. As each of these phases of development is accomplished, the overall value of the property increases. When the project is completed and ready to produce income or be sold, it will be refinanced by a permanent lender.

A bank or institutional investor may finance any one or all of the phases of a real estate project. Most of the permanent financing, however, is provided by institutional lenders and investors with longer investment horizons than banks, such as insurance companies, pension funds, and real estate investment trusts.

Banks usually prefer to finance the initial land development and construction phases of a real estate project over the (relatively) shorter term. They also provide short-term financing for completed projects. These so-called "mini-perm" loans are used when the developer intends to sell the project soon after normal occupancy levels are achieved. The miniperm loan allows the developer to avoid the cost and work associated with obtaining a permanent loan commitment prior to completing the project. Miniperm loans, however, have also been common in distressed periods for commercial real estate, such as the early 1990s, when they reflected developers' inability to obtain permanent financing. The "involuntary" miniperm loans of that period were often part of a bank's work-out strategy for its troubled commercial real estate construction and development sectors.

Credit Risk (Or Why Construction Loans Are So Complex)

Credit risk is the risk to earnings or capital arising from an obligor's failure to meet the terms of any contract with the lender or otherwise failing to perform as agreed. Credit risk is found in all activities where success depends on counterparty, issuer, or borrower performance. It arises any time lender funds are extended, committed, invested, or otherwise exposed through actual or implied contractual agreements, whether reflected on or off the balance sheet.

Given the nature of most commercial real estate markets, the financing of commercial real estate projects is subject to an exceptionally high degree of credit risk. The limited supply of land at a given commercially attractive location, the exceptionally long economic life of the assets, the very long delivery timeframes required for the development and construction of major projects, and high interest rate sensitivity have given commercial real estate markets a long history of extreme cyclical fluctuations and volatility.

The table below delineates the steps and documentation required to do a construction loan. This table also provides an excellent illustration of the complexity of project or construction loans.

Information Required to Apply for a Construction Loan

I. General Information Required

A. Financial statements for past three years and/or pro forma statements based on completion of project. Include cash-flow projections.
B. Property description, location, and cost information.
C. Loan request:
    1. Amount
    2. Term
    3. Interest rate and fees
    4. Repayment schedule
    5. Prepayment
    6. Tax and insurance deposits
    7. Disbursement procedure - One payout, progress payments, or voucher system?
    8. Lien information (existing)

II. Contractor Information Required

A. Names of general contractor and subcontractors.
B. Actual or estimated cost calculations.
C. Copy of plans and specifications.
D. Copy of construction contract, if executed.
E. All pertinent bonding information.

Information Required to Apply for a Construction Loan

III. Loan Analysis

IV. Borrower

  A. Review of historical financial information plus pro forma.

  B. Credit check of borrower through Dun & Bradstreet and bank of account.

  C. Management experience (is continuity a problem?)

  D. Ratio of project cash flow to debt-servicing requirements.

  E. Analysis of project effect on working capital in regard to other commitments.

  F. Ability to meet unexpected contingencies.

  G. Need for personal guarantees—usually required unless construction loan agreement covenants provide acceptable substitutes, or unless past experience makes it unnecessary.

V. Property and improvements

  A. Appraisal of market value of land.

  B. Review of existing encumbrances on land. Beware of:

    1. Use of part of loan to purchase or pay encumbrances on the land.

      a. Purchase-money mortgages on land (borrower must have this subordinated; consider repayment capabilities in regard to two mortgages).

    2. Analysis of building costs and land improvements.

    3. Review of local zoning laws and building codes applicable to the project.

    4. If construction costs should exceed amount of loan, and if borrower should deposit difference with the lender.

    5. Appraisal of property based on market value when completed.

  C. Contractor and construction

    1. Analysis of reputation of general contractor and significant subcontractors (Dun & Bradstreet reports).

    2. Construction contract should be executed before funds are advanced.

      a. Plans and specifications should be prepared on final working drawings, not preliminaries, by architect or engineer, along with a trade payment breakdown (construction budget).

      b. Independent architect or professional engineer should be employed at borrower's expense to approve progress payments

Information Required to Apply for a Construction Loan

and assure compliance with agreed-upon specifications.

   c. Selection of one bonded general contractor. Where general contractor and developer are one and the same, subcontractors would be bonded.

   d. Bonded contracts should embrace plans and specifications that are contemplated, particularly concerning outside improvements.

   e. Maximums should be set on estimated costs.

   f. Time requirements should be explicit.

   g. No substantial changes should be made without consent of all parties.

D. Bonds

   1. Furnished by corporate surety acceptable to lenders, naming contractor as principal, borrower as obligee, and lender as dual obligee. Penalty is full contract amount.

   2. Types

      a. Completion bond—strongest; guarantees improvements will be completed by certain time.

      b. Performance bond—promises to stand behind agreement of contractor, provided owner performs all covenants with contractor.

      c. Payment bonds—guarantees all materialmen's and subcontractor's payment fees and clear of lien; may be included in other bonds.

   3. Independent verification of bonding company should be obtained regarding validity and effectiveness of executed bond.

   4. Bond requirements can be waived in case of materialmen, but retained when significant labor is involved.

   5. Requirement usually dependent on size of loan, location of project, credit worthiness of borrower, and knowledge of reputation through experience.

   6. Alternative to lender's being named dual obligee: assignment of borrower's interest in bond.

E. Takeout commitment

   1. Analysis of intent of lender—standby letter is issued for fee only or full intention to fund upon completion. Determined by:

      a. Amount of fee paid for issuance (over one percent is suspect).

Information Required to Apply for a Construction Loan

      b. Insistence of buy-sell agreement.

      c. Terms of end loan (should be conventional as to rate and term).

      d. Commitment enforceable upon completion or for extended period of time.

    2. Analysis of takeout commitment letter—should have certification of no unknown provisions affecting transaction between borrower and end lender.

    3. Size and reputation of end lender should be considered.

    4. Commitment should be firm in regard to plans and specifications, title, construction timetable, certificate of occupancy, and rent-up requirements.

    5. Availability of agreement by end lender to extend commitment.

    6. Review of requirements by end lender to extend commitment.

  F. The loan request

    1. Feasibility of project—possibility always exists that through unforeseen occurrences lender could own the project.

    2. Funds required—cash flow essential. Must include:

      a. Reserve for charges—add sixty-day period beyond builder's estimate for closing of ending loan; estimate charges to be incurred.

      b. Reserve for contingencies—usually 10 percent of total costs.

VI. Commitment Letter Contents

  A. Description of loan

    1. Amount.

    2. Term, including cancellation and extension rights.

    3. Interest rate and service charges or loan fees.

    4. Right of prepayment.

  B. First and second liens

    1. Mortgage or deed of trust as first lien.

    2. Conventional secondary financing is normally forbidden.

  [Subsidy financing from federal, state or local governments is ordinarily permitted if it is subordinate.]

  C. Recordation—forms customarily used:

    1. Note.

    2. Mortgage or deed of trust.

    3. Construction loan agreement.

    4. Assignment of rents.

Information Required to Apply for a Construction Loan

    5. Borrower's receipt.

    6. Tenant's acceptance statements.

    7. Estoppel certificates.

    8. Personal guarantees.

    9. Security interests in personal property.

D. No assignment of commitment without lender's approval

E. Evidence of title

    1. Title insurance to be required.

    2. Satisfactory evidence of title.

F. Plans and specifications—must conform to those used in making appraisal of commitment.

G. Compliance with:

    1. Zoning laws.

    2. Building code requirements, notwithstanding issuance of a building permit.

H. Assignment of leases—collateral assignments as they are entered into.

I. Permanent mortgage commitment–certification of compliance with same.

J. Insurance

    1. Lender named as loss payee and co-insured.

    2. Specification of:

        a. Fire and extended coverage with standard mortgage clause.

        b. Liability.

        c. Business interruption.

        d. Builder's-risk nonreporting.

        e. Rent loss.

        f. Workmen's compensation payments during construction period.

        g. Performance or completion bonds.

K. Loan holdback

    1. Final portion of loan (10 to 15 percent) will not be disbursed until final completion.

    2. Completion evidenced by:

        a. Architect's certificate.

        b. Permanent certificate of occupancy. [In some cases a temporary certificate of occupancy may be acceptable.]

Information Required to Apply for a Construction Loan

    L. Opening of loan—conditions required prior to loan opening:
        1. Stage of completion.
        2. Deposit of difference between loan and total construction cost.
        3. Waiver of mechanic's lien.
    M. Progress payments—conditions to be met before disbursements.
    N. Payments to general contractor:
        1. Made upon waiver of subcontractors' liens.
        2. Made directly to subcontractor.
    O. Interest computation
    P. Agreement to employ independent architect or professional engineer
    Q. Acceptance of commitment—period within which borrower must accept commitment.

VII. Execution of Documents

See "recordation," above, for listing of documents that may need to be executed.

VIII. Recording Documents to Perfect Lender's Lien

IX. Title Examination

X. Loan Disbursements Procedure
    A. Loan disbursement statement
        1. Total amount of loan.
        2. Itemized deductions.
            a. Service charges.
            b. Title expense.
            c. Legal expenses.
            d. Appraisal fees.
            e. Credit reports.
            f. Tax and insurance reserves.
        3. Net amount available for construction.
        4. Borrower's signature.
    B. Examination of contractor's sworn statement.
        1. Check accuracy of construction contract.
        2. Possibility of direct verification with subcontractors.
    C. Form of mechanic's lien waivers.
        1. Name of subcontractor and work performed.
        2. Total contract amount, amount requested, and balance due.
        3. Affidavit stating amounts still due.

As you can clearly see from the previous table, a construction loan is a complicated loan to originate! Because of this, a construction loan uses a hard money lender.

Hard Money Loans

Purchasing or Refinancing With a Hard Money Mortgage

Hard money comes in many flavors; one of the most common is mortgages. Using the owner's equity in real estate, hard money lenders generally lend 65% to 70% of the value of real estate property. In general, hard money mortgages are used for commercial purposes. However, they can also be applied to residential properties. In this instance, the loan is generally referred to by its more genteel name: a nonconforming mortgage.

Lending criteria for hard money mortgages are fairly simple. The loan is based on the value of the 'subject property.' If the borrower is buying the subject property, the value of the real estate is defined as the actual purchase price of the property.

If the borrower already owns the subject property but needs hard money for a refinance situation, the value is determined by a written real estate appraisal.

If you are a borrower looking for a hard money refinance loan, the lender will want to know when you purchased the property and what you paid for it. If you bought the property less than a year ago, the lender will be disinclined to lend you more than your original purchase price. Once you've owned the property for about a year, especially if you have put some money, sweat equity, or both into the property, you can get a new appraisal and a loan based on the new, improved value of the property. This is called 'seasoning' the property. Be sure the property is seasoned for about a year before seeking to refinance a mortgage at a significantly higher value than the actual purchase price.

Why is hard money so important in real estate investing? There are several reasons. Real estate investing is a cash intensive financial activity. In order to take advantage of ongoing projects, investors often require more operating capital than conventional banks are prepared to provide on short notice. To further complicate matters, if you invest in a lot of property, your FICO score can plummet simply due to the number of mortgages you owe! Conventional financing may not be available to an investor with low FICO scores. Additionally, the properties that can be had for an advantageous price may not meet conventional banking criteria. Thus, because hard money lenders are not restricted in the same way conventional banks are when it comes to real estate investing, hard money can be a deal saver.

Hard money lenders can turn on a dime. Mortgages for real estate investing can take anywhere from two to six months to be completed by conventional banks and lenders. Hard money lenders can generally fund within two weeks once you have all the paperwork in place. Hard money lenders can also fund projects that conventional lenders cannot. Loans for projects like a dry cleaners (or a strip mall that houses one), a gas station, an assisted living facility, a golf course, or a marina are all difficult to accomplish through conventional lenders. Such projects are much more likely to be funded by hard money lenders.

Hard money is best used as a bridge loan to acquire the property and make improvements. Terms generally range from one to three years. This provides an ample time frame for the borrower to prepare the property and/or his personal financial status in order to arrange for long-term conventional financing.

Alternatively, this one- to three-year time period allows the borrower to arrange for the sale of the property.

Another reason to seek a hard money loan is to prevent foreclosure on the property. Such loans are the specialty that brings out the best and the worst in hard money lenders. If your client is facing foreclosure on a property, hard money lenders may be your only resource for sufficient cash in a timely manner.

Hard money lenders can fund a real estate purchase or refinance loan in as little as two weeks from the time all your documentation is in their hands. It is even possible to get it done in less time. I once did a hard money loan in only two days. This was possible because I had all of the documentation prepared for the lender, and because I had developed a trusting relationship with this lender over the years. So be sure to have all your documentation ready for the lender in order to keep the turnaround time short. The following list is a guideline for the documentation you should prepare for the hard money lender. (Note: If you do not have a current appraisal, you must at least provide an old one, or the process will be delayed.)

Documents to Provide to Hard Money Lenders

- Written real estate appraisal with photos

- Purchase contract (if you are purchasing the property)

- Personal financial statement

- Income statement for the borrower

- Two years P&L for the property if it is income-producing

- Two years Tax returns for the borrower

- Statement of use of funds

- Proof of where the balance of funding will come from (such as a bank statement showing the funds available) if you are buying the property

Being prepared with a complete package will speed your funding.

Bridge Loans

The best financing tool for some difficult situations

Bridge loans are loans with a short "term." A bridge loan's terms range from just a few days to as long as five years. A great example of a bridge loan is the corner blue-collar pay day Lender that lends money to individuals against their next paycheck. In commercial real estate, bridge loans are used to enable a quick closing, allowing the borrower to take advantage of an opportunity and arrange for longer term financing at his or her leisure.

Real estate bridge loans are used for both purchases and refinancing. Speed is often of paramount importance in bridge loans.

Investors in income-producing commercial real estate are frequently required to manage certain challenges that impact net income, value or both. Some investors see these challenges as problems, while others see the same challenges as opportunities. These problems or opportunities include:

- High vacancy
- Incomplete financial reports
- Change of use
- Receivership
- Poor physical condition
- Debt buy-down opportunity
- Lack of adequate seasoning
- Debtor-in-possession
- Foreclosure
- Partnership liquidation
- Chapter 11 bankruptcy filing

An owner facing the above problems is probably also facing an immediate need to refinance due to a maturing loan. For a purchaser seeking below-market values, the other investor's problems becomes his opportunity to make a below-market acquisition. In any of the above situations, a bridge loan may be the best or, perhaps, the only option.

Here is a quick look at some bridge loan basics:

A bridge loan is a short-term loan on a property that, for various reasons, does not (yet) qualify for a conventional or permanent loan. Generally, bridge loans are risky for the lender. The property is the primary collateral for the loan, but as a result of various problems, the property may not be financially stabilized. Often, historical and current revenues will not support traditional lending criteria. The "hair" on the deal will range widely, meaning you, as the broker, will have to address a wide range of problems. The problems plaguing the loan may involve the property, the borrower, or the transaction itself. Often, the problems involve a combination of all three.

The SBA 504 Program 50-40-10

The Small Business Association's CDC/504 loan program is a long-term financing tool for economic development within a community. The 504 program provides growing businesses with long-term, fixed-rate financing for major fixed assets, such as land and buildings. A Certified Development Company (CDC) is a nonprofit corporation set up to contribute to the economic development of its community. CDCs work with the Small Business Association (SBA) to private-sector financing for small businesses. There are about 270 CDCs nationwide. Each CDC covers a specific geographic area. **Some lenders have special relationships with CDCs and, accordingly, you should work with them.**

Typically, a 504 project includes a loan secured with a senior lien from a private-sector lender covering up to 50 percent of the project cost, a loan secured with a junior lien from the CDC (backed by a 100 percent SBA-guaranteed debenture) covering up to 40 percent of the cost, and a contribution of at least 10 percent equity from the small business being helped.

Maximum Debenture

The maximum SBA debenture is dependent on the goal/criteria for the loan.

The maximum debenture is $1,500,000 if the borrower meets the job creation criteria or other community development goal. Generally, a business must create or retain one job for every $50,000 provided by the SBA, except for "small manufacturers," which have a $100,000 job creation or retention goal (see below).

The maximum SBA debenture is $2 million when meeting a public policy goal. The public policy goals are as follows:

- Business district revitalization

- Expansion of exports

- Expansion of minority business development

- Rural development

- Increasing productivity and competitiveness

- Restructuring because of federally mandated standards or policies

- Changes necessitated by federal budget cutbacks

- Expansion of small business concerns owned and controlled by veterans (especially service-disabled veterans)

- Expansion of small business concerns owned and controlled by women

The maximum debenture for small manufacturers is $4 million. A small manufacturer is defined as a small business concern that has:

1. Its primary business classified in sector 31, 32, or 33 of the North American Industrial Classification System (NAICS); and

2. All of its production facilities located in the United States.

In order to qualify for a $4 million 504 loan, the small manufacturer must 1) meet the definition of a small manufacturer described above, and 2) either (i) create or retain at least 1 job per $100,000 guaranteed by the SBA [Section 501(d)(1) of the Small Business Investment Act (SBI Act)], or (ii) improve the economy of the locality or achieve one or more public policy goals [sections 501(d)(2) or (3) of the SBI Act].

Use of SBA 504 Funds

Proceeds from 504 loans must be used for fixed asset projects such as: purchasing land and improvements including existing buildings, grading, street improvements, utilities, parking lots, and landscaping; construction of new facilities, or modernizing, renovating, or converting existing facilities; or purchasing long-term machinery and equipment. The 504 program cannot be used for working capital or inventory, consolidating or repaying debt, or refinancing.

Terms, Interest Rates and Fees

Interest rates on 504 loans are pegged to an increment above the current market rate for 5-year and 10-year U.S. Treasury issues. Maturities of 10 and 20 years are available. Fees total approximately three (3) percent of the debenture and may be financed with the loan.

Collateral

Generally, the project assets being financed are used as collateral. Personal guaranties of the principal owners are also required.

Eligible Businesses

To be eligible, the business must be operated for profit and fall within the size standards set by the SBA. Under the 504 program, the business qualifies as small if it does not have a tangible net worth in excess of $7 million and does not have an average net income in excess of $2.5 million after taxes for the preceding two years. Loans cannot be made to businesses engaged in speculation or investment in rental real estate.

To determine if you qualify for SBA's financial assistance, you should first understand some basic credit factors that apply to all loan requests. Every application needs positive credit merits to be approved. A lender will review and analyze the following five credit factors before deciding whether to internally approve your loan application, seek a guaranty from SBA to support their loan to you, or decline your application altogether.

1. Equity Investment

Business loan applicants must have a reasonable amount invested in their business. This ensures that, when combined with borrowed funds, the business can operate on a sound basis. There will be a careful examination of the debt-to-worth ratio of the applicant to understand how much money the lender is being asked to lend (debt) in relation to how much the owner(s) have invested (worth). Owner investment is defined as assets that apply to the business' operation, and/or cash that can be used to acquire such assets. The value of invested assets should be substantiated by invoices or appraisals for start-up businesses, or current financial statements for existing businesses.

Strong equity with a manageable debt level provides financial resiliency to help a firm weather periods of operational adversity. Minimal or nonexistent equity increases the risk of defaulting on the loan. Strong equity ensures the owner(s) remains committed to the business. Sufficient equity is particularly important for a new business. Weak equity makes a lender more hesitant to provide any financial assistance. However, low (not nonexistent) equity can be overcome in relation to the SBA 504 loan with a strong showing in all the other credit factors.

Determining whether a company's level of debt is appropriate in relation to its equity requires analysis of the company's expected earnings and the viability and variability of these earnings. The stronger the support for projected profits, the greater the likelihood the loan will be approved. Applications with high debt, low equity, and unsupported projections are prime candidates for loan denial.

2. Earnings Requirements

Financial obligations are paid with cash, not profits. When cash outflow exceeds cash inflow for an extended period of time, a business cannot continue to operate. As a result, cash management is extremely important. In order to adequately support a company's operation, cash must be at the right place, at the right time and in the right amount.

A company must be able to meet all its debt payments, not just its loan payments, as they come due. Applicants are generally required to provide a report on when their income will become cash and when their expenses must be paid. This report is usually in the form of a cash flow projection, broken down on a monthly basis, and covering the first annual period after the loan is received.

When the monthly cash flow projections are for either a new business or an existing business with a significant (20% plus) difference in performance, the applicant should write down all assumptions that went into the estimations of both revenues and expenses and provide these assumptions as part of the application.

All SBA loans must be able to reasonably demonstrate the "ability to repay" the intended obligation from the business operation. For an existing business wanting to buy a building where the mortgage payment will not exceed historical rent, the process is relatively easy. In this case, the funds used to pay the rent can now be used to pay the mortgage. However, for a new or expanding business with anticipated revenues and expenses exceeding past performance, the necessity for the lender to understand all the assumptions on how these revenues will be generated is paramount to loan approval.

3. Working Capital

Working capital is defined as the excess of current assets over current liabilities.

Current assets are the most liquid of all assets, the most easily convertible to cash. Current liabilities are obligations due within one year. Therefore, working capital measures what is available to pay a company's current debts. It also represents the cushion or margin of protection a company can give its short term creditors.

Working capital is essential for a company to meet its continuous operational needs. Its adequacy influences the firm's ability to meet its trade and short-term debt obligations, as well as to remain financially viable.

4. Collateral

To the extent that worthwhile assets are available, adequate collateral is required as security on all SBA loans. However, SBA will generally not decline a loan where inadequacy of collateral is the only unfavorable factor.

Collateral can consist of both assets that are usable in the business and personal assets which remain outside the business. Borrowers can assume that all assets financed with borrowed funds will collateralize the loan. Depending upon how much equity was contributed towards the acquisition of these assets, the lender also is likely to require other business assets as collateral.

For all SBA loans, personal guarantees are required of every 20% or greater owner, plus others individuals who hold key management positions. Whether or not a guarantee will be secured by personal assets is based on the value of the assets already pledged and the value of the assets personally owned compared to the amount borrowed. In the event real estate is to be used as collateral, borrowers should be aware that banks and other regulated lenders are now required by law to obtain third-party valuation on real estate-related transactions of $50,000 or more.

Certified appraisals are required for loans of $100,000 or more. SBA may require professional appraisals of both business and personal assets, plus any necessary survey(s), and/or a feasibility study.

Owner-occupied residences generally become collateral when:

1) The lender requires the residence as collateral

2) The equity in the residence is substantial and other credit factors are weak

3) Such collateral is necessary to assure that the principal(s) remain committed to the success of the venture for which the loan is being made

4) The applicant operates the business out of the residence or other buildings located on the same parcel of land

5. Resource Management

The ability of individuals to manage the resources of their business, sometimes referred to as "character," is a prime consideration when determining whether or not a loan will be made. Managerial capacity is an important factor involving education, experience and motivation. A proven positive ability to manage resources is also a large consideration.

Mathematical calculations on the historical and projected financial statements form ratios that provide insight into how resources have been managed in the past. It is important to understand that no single ratio provides all this insight, but the use of several ratios in conjunction with one another can provide an overall picture of management performance. Some key ratios all lenders review are: debt to worth, working capital, the rate at which income is received after it is earned, the rate at which debt is paid after becoming due, and the rate at which the service or product moves from the business to the customer.

These five key characteristics which lenders study for SBA loans are similar to the type of information and assurances which all private lenders seek, regardless of the loan type. In the loan packaging software provided on the *CRES Solutions* CD, all of these lender concerns are addressed. As you will see in Chapter 7, the software has a heading and input field for each significant area of concern. The credit approval presentation in Chapter 7 guides you through each of these areas, giving tips and suggestions for putting together a loan package that adequately address these common lender concerns.

As you can see, the type of loan you should seek for your client will vary. Borrower goals, lender criteria, the amount of time and information available to you, and your client's financial profile will all substantially impact the type of deal you seek.

CHAPTER FIVE

Working with Real Estate Appraisals

The Appraisal's Role in the Financing

An appraisal is a written opinion of real estate value as of a specific date. When prepared by a qualified appraiser, it represents an independent and impartial analysis of all the relevant data. Because market value is not apparent just from a visual inspection, an appraisal is usually required when a property is sold, taxed, insured, or financed.

Licensed appraisers must adhere to the Uniform Standards of Professional Appraisal Practice (USPAP), which became effective in 1993. These rules have established a high level of professional and ethical standards that all licensed appraisers must follow.

Industry standard forms are used for most residential appraisals, but narrative reports are prepared for commercial properties. All appraisal reports contain facts and analyses of the subject property, the neighborhood, and the market. The reports include rent roll information as of the date of the appraisal, and income and expenses for the property for both year-to-date and previous year. Commercial appraisals contain exhibits, including photographs of the subject and comparable properties, a detailed scale sketch of the subject, a map showing the subject in relation to the comparables, and a flood plane map showing the subject property. All appraisal reports contain a Statement of Limiting Conditions and an Appraiser's Certification.

Appraisal Market Value

The appraisal report includes information on the area economy; factors that influence neighborhood market value; characteristics of the site, including any improvements thereon; and identification/analysis of any other factors that might impact the value of the subject property.

Three approaches to value are employed:

1. Cost Approach: This approach is based on the proposition that the informed purchaser would pay no more than the cost of producing a substitute property with the same utility as the subject property. It is particularly applicable when the property being appraised involves relatively new improvements that represent the highest and best use of the land or when unique or specialized improvements are located on the market. This method involves estimating the reproduction cost of the new improvements, then subtracting accrued depreciation from all sources. To this is added the market value of the land, which has been found by direct sales comparison (below). In fast growing areas with restricted land availability, the value of the land may surpass the value of the structure as area redevelopment takes place.

2. Direct Sales Comparison: This approach is based on the proposition that an informed purchaser would pay no more for a property than the cost to him of acquiring an existing property with the same utility. This approach is applicable when an active market provides sufficient quantities of reliable data that can be verified. This involves comparing the subject property to actual sales of similar properties, with appropriate adjustments made for any differences between the properties. Various unit values are developed which, when applied to like units of the subject, give an indication of value for the subject.

3. Income Approach: This is the procedure that converts anticipated benefits (dollar income or amenities) derived from ownership of the property into a value estimate. This technique relates to the future benefits arising out of property ownership, such as current and anticipated future income. The benefits are estimated by deducting fixed and operating expenses from the gross potential annual income, to arrive at the net operating income that is required to attract capital to the property.

Reconciliation:

Reconciliation is the process by which the appraiser evaluates, chooses and selects from among two or more alternative conclusions or indications to reach a single valuation.

Once an indication of value has been determined independently with each of the approaches above, the three approaches are then correlated into a single conclusion of value. This value judgment is based on the reliability (highest quantity and quality of data available) of each approach and the one that is most pertinent to the objectives of the investor (e.g. if a property is desired for its income-producing potential, then the indication of value by the income approach would be of particular interest to the prospective purchaser).

Style, age, overall condition, square footage, and quality of construction are also important. Other factors that influence market value, such as neighborhood, location, proximity to major streets or highway zoning, comparable sales, design, and floor plans are also considered. More complex criteria, including income and expense data, condition of improvements, and replacement costs, are considered as well.

Due to the infrequency at which commercial properties of similar type trade, the appraiser must adjust value by allocating a monthly value increase to comparables in markets where property values are increasing at a fast pace, as has happened in some Florida and California markets during the last five years.

Commercial and multifamily lenders usually require that all three methods be provided in an appraisal.

The appraiser calculates the increase in value over the months since the last comparable transaction (comp) and applies that to the selling price, giving the lender and the borrower a better idea of value for the subject property.

The adjusted comps and the resulting appraisal value of the subject property are sometimes a subject of much dispute between the borrower, the lender and the appraised. These issues can blow up a deal. Here in South Florida, where the writer resides, we have done transactions where the purchase price of the subject property was $160 per square foot and the last transaction of a comparable was 11 months earlier at $90 per square foot. The appraiser came up with a valuation of $130 per square foot. Since our lender was lending 85% of the purchase price or the appraised value, the significantly lower valuation required the buyer to come up with additional capital for the down payment. A major battle of words ensued between the borrower and the appraiser. The borrower hired a new appraiser, but, due to time constraints in the purchase contract, the buyer was in a bind.

Then came the white knight, a condo converter from New York with deep pockets who I had contacted. He offered to buy the purchase contract from our buyer/borrower for $170 per square foot. The deal was done with the existing appraisal because the new buyer had deep pockets. After the conversion was done, the resulting condos sold for $300 per square foot. Needless to say the original buyer is still fuming over that. The lesson on this story is that, as the broker, you have to review each appraisal as it comes in, before the appraisal goes to the lender. Your only opportunity to question the appraiser if the appraisal is lower than the purchase price is *before* you send the appraisal to the lender. Once you have sent on the appraisal to the lender, there is no way out. The second lesson is to try and work with borrowers who are financially strong and have good credit. The concept of buying commercial property with no money down does not apply here.

Be careful with appraisals and appraisers; when you select an appraiser, be sure he or she holds the MAI designation and is competent to appraise the type of property and market for which your client is seeking financing. An out of town appraiser will always be conservative, and that is reflected in his final valuation, which then affects your loan.

We are entering a period of rising interest rates; the higher the rates go, the lower the values of the properties go because the debt service coverage gets affected by high interest rate payments. Therefore, in the next few years you have to be very careful in structuring the loans to ensure your DSCR is somewhat above your minimum; this gives you some leeway to allow for the effect of rising rates between the times the application is put in until the time you can LOCK the rate.

If your investor allows you to order appraisals, make sure you know the investor's appraisal requirements very well and communicate those requirements to the appraiser, in writing, when you send the engagement letter. Make sure you get a copy of the engagement letter once it has been signed and accepted by the appraiser. Our *CRES Solutions* CD contains a typical engagement letter for your use. It also contains, for your reference, the appraisal requirements of one of the largest commercial lenders in the industry.

CHAPTER SIX

Multifamily Underwriting Guidelines

Now that we have discussed types of loans and lenders, it is time to prepare you to underwrite an appealing loan package to entice a prospective lender. The next two chapters will introduce you to the basic underwriting of the two major sectors of commercial mortgage finance.

These two major sectors are multifamily (apartment buildings) and commercial.

They are also the only two sectors for which you can obtain loans on a stated basis.

Remember, stated loans make it easier for your clients to move quickly when purchasing or expanding their business. After a detailed review of both the multifamily and the owner-occupied underwriting guidelines in Chapters 6 and 7, Chapter 8 will show you how to do multifamily and owner-occupied on a stated basis. Subsequent chapters are dedicated to providing the underwriting guidelines for the other commercial mortgage finance sectors (e.g., office, retail, hotel/motel), which must be underwritten as full documentation loans, rather than stated basis loans.

The *CRES Solutions* CD contains all of the forms you will need to input and calculate the underwriting guidelines detailed below. I will refer to the CD throughout this discussion and provide instructions for using the CD to prepare the loan package. Before we begin discussing apartment underwriting guidelines, allow me to overview the basic steps you will need to take to prepare the loan package. Keep these in mind as you read this chapter:

- Obtain a completed rent roll
- Obtain property income and expenses for the year to date
- Obtain property income and expenses for the last two years

• Then enter all the above information into one of the credit memo forms provided on the CD. The software will do the rest of the work for you!

Sounds easy, but of course you'll want to know what lenders look for in a good apartment loan so you'll be able to look at your finished loan package and evaluate its strengths and weaknesses. This chapter is dedicated to explaining loan analysis from the lender's point of view. You'll have a much stronger chance of getting your client's loan funded once you understand what the lenders look for and why certain characteristics are more desirable than others.

So, let's get started with apartments. One of the biggest sectors of commercial mortgages is the purchase financing or refinancing of multi-unit apartment buildings. To qualify as a commercial multifamily apartment building, a building must have at least five apartments. If a building has only four apartments, it must be financed under residential rules. Licensing requirements apply to transactions considered to be residential. Therefore, do not finance any four-unit buildings unless you are licensed as a residential mortgage broker or correspondent lender.

The properties that qualify as multifamily include: low-rise garden apartment, mid-rise apartment, military housing, low-student housing, townhouse style, co-op, other apartment, and mobile home park.

Apartment Underwriting Profile

In order to obtain funding, an apartment loan package should reflect the following key characteristics:

• Most lenders lend a maximum of 80% LTV (Loan to Value) on apartments. A few lenders, including my own company, Coast Investors, lend up to 85% LTV, provided the borrower has good credit. The exceptions to this rule of thumb are student and military housing. Typically student and military housing have shorter lease terms than other apartment types, resulting in a lower LTV. For student or military housing, the LTV ranges from 75% to 80%.

• The typical amortization ranges from 25 to 30 years. For student and military housing, reduce this to 25 years.

• Minimum DSCR ranges from 1.20x to 1.25x. A higher DSCR is required for student and military housing; typically 1.25x to 1.30x.

• Minimum vacancy reserve should reflect the greater of actual or market vacancy; typically 3% to 10%. Student and military housing ranges from 5% to 10%.

• Minimum replacement reserves will be the greater of actual or $225-$350 per unit. Again, student and military housing are the exceptions. For student/military, use the greater of actual or $300-$400 per unit to calculate NOI.

• Minimum occupancy requirement is typically 85%. This requirement is more stringent for student and military housing, requiring at least 85% occupancy over the past two years.

• Capitalization rate—use market-driven capitalization rate, typically 7.5% to 10%. Where an apartment building is being purchased for the purpose of converting it to a condominium and then selling the individual units, do not seek an apartment loan since you will not be allowed to sell the units one at the time. Instead, look for a lender that does condo conversion loans as described in a later chapter.

• Student and military housing leases must require 12-month terms and parental guarantee; however, exceptions can be obtained to this rule. I have seen many transactions funded with leases of 8 and 9 months.

The easiest way to prepare an attractive loan package according to these guidelines is to utilize the forms provided on the *CRES Solutions* CD. The software will guide you through the information collection and calculation process. Your awareness of the above key factors will assist you in entering the correct information into the software. Additionally, the next chapter provides you with a step-by-step example of how to prepare the pertinent data and what information to input into the software. If you are not using the CD software, you will still need to calculate and provide all of the same information. Keep in mind that new brokers may want to utilize the loan preparation services offered at *www.cresguide.com*. If you are wholly new to commercial real estate mortgage brokering, I recommend that you partner with the professionals at *cresguide.com* until you feel comfortable preparing the loan packages yourself. You can earn while you learn, and by utilizing our database of potential lenders, you can also begin creating relationships with these lenders for the future.

General Guidelines

Market and Location

The property being submitted for a loan should be within a reasonable distance (defined as a 3-mile radius) of retail services such as grocery stores, drugstores, and a community shopping center. The property should be within a 10-mile radius of community services such as fire, police, schools, and health facilities.

Properties located in economically depressed, seasonal or resort-oriented areas are more difficult to finance due to higher vacancy rates, higher turnover, lower income, and lower value growth.

Where a property has a high percentage of corporate rental leases (over 10%), the accounts must be high credit, long-term accounts with stable histories, higher reserve amounts (due to furniture rentals), and higher spreads.

No more than 25% of the total units should have leases set to expire within any given month; no more than 50% of the units should expire within any 3-month period, and no more than 75% for any 6-month period.

Property Condition and Characteristics

A property should have an appropriate mix of units to remain competitive in its market. Properties with more than three stories should have elevator service. An exception to this elevator rule would be a market with many older buildings, where "walk-ups" are common and in high demand.

In suburban markets, look for a minimum parking ratio of 1.0 spaces for studio/efficiency and 1 bedroom units, 1.5 spaces for 2 bedroom units, and 2.0 spaces for 3+ bedroom units. Urban areas require adequate parking in order for the property to compete successfully.

Properties should exhibit acceptable aesthetic qualities to be competitive with market standards. Inferior physical characteristics are obviously less desirable and may require a higher interest rate spread and higher underwriting constraints and reserves.

Normalizing Income and Expense Considerations

Calculate Potential Gross Income (PGI) by adding the annual in-place revenue generated by the current tenants to the annual income generated from vacant space at market rent. Then apply the appropriate vacancy reserve to the PGI to calculate effective gross income.

Income is typically calculated based on the actual revenue collected during the most recent 12-month period or per a current rent roll certified by the borrower.

In order to obtain the most reliable figure, you may need to make some further adjustments. If any of the property's leases are written above or below market rent (e.g., if a tenant pays $500/unit/month although the market rent for comparable properties is $350/unit/month), then you will want to mark that lease at market rate ($350 in our example) to normalize the figure. Delinquent tenants are another issue to consider. You might choose to subtract rental income from any tenant who is 60 days or more delinquent.

Finally, review storage, parking, laundry, and any other income listed to make sure it is consistent with the historical income generated by the property for the past two years.

Vacancy and Collection Loss

To determine vacancy and collection loss factors, the underwriter reviews the following two sources and uses whichever source results in the greater number. The first source is the current market or economic vacancy rate listed in *Black's Guide* (see Chapter 2, "Qualifying a Lead" section for the *Black's Guide* web link.) The second source is the actual collection losses at the property over the past two years. Compare these sources to determine which gives you the highest vacancy and collection loss figure.

Additional factors that influence the vacancy and collection loss figure are the creditworthiness of the existing tenant base and the number of short-term or month-to-month leases. Furthermore, the underwriter will review any other factors that might impact the ability to collect future rents.

Historical Review

When analyzing income and expense trends, explain any significant increase or decrease over 5% per annum. Certain adjustments to the expenses may include increasing or decreasing or normalizing the underwritten expenses based upon historical expense trends.

The management fee will be the same whether the property is professionally managed or owner-managed. Apply the greater of the actual management fee, or the market management fee; typically this will give you a figure ranging from 3% to 5%.

Apply an expense growth-rate of 3% to represent escalation of expenses for the next 12 months. Remove any insurance expense that is not specifically related to the real estate, such as personal health insurance.

Remove any nonrecurring expenses from the underwritten expense. Reallocate any capital expenses from Repairs & maintenance to capital expenditures.

Rent Roll Form

One of the key documents in securing financing for a multifamily project is the rent roll. The rent roll is a document that list all the units in a building, the name of the lessee, when the lease begins and ends, the size of the unit, the amount being paid, and the market rental price for similar units. The borrower must provide all of the information for this form, and then the borrower should sign the completed form to certify that the rent roll is true and correct.

The easiest way to prepare an accurate rent roll is to utilize the rent roll form provided on the *CRES Solutions* CD. This is what the rent roll form looks like:

Multifamily Rent Role											
Rent Roll as of : 1/0/00 (required)											

Property Address		City		State	Zip						
Total Number of Units: 0		Number of Vacant Units: 0		Number of Furnished Units: 0		Number of Unfurnished Units: 0		Number of Section 8 Units: 0			
Apt. #	Tenant's Name	BDR/ Bath	SQ. Feet (approx)	Current Rent In Place	Market Rent	Original Occupancy Date	Current Lease Expiration or MTM	Date Last Rent Increase	Furnished Unit (Y/N)	Sec 8 (Y/N)	Rent Concessions

The steps to completing the rent roll form are simple:

The rent roll form

1. **Tenant Name:** Enter the name of the tenant.

2. **Contract Rent:** This is the actual rent

3. **Market Rent:** Enter the estimated market rent. Get average for your area from *Apartmentguide.com*

4. **Sq. Feet (Leased Area):** Enter the leased area in square feet.

5. **Occupancy Date:** Enter the month/ year of occupancy by current renter.

6. **Lease Expiration:** Enter the actual lease expiration date.

7. **Date Last Rent Increase:** Enter date if applicable.

8. **Furnished Unit:** Lenders want to know if there are furnished units. Furnished apartments are an indicator of low income, short term or transient rental units.

9. **Section 8:** This is the government assisted rent program.

10. Rent Concession: Does the owner or other entity help pay for the renter's rent?

Once you have the rent roll, your income and expenses for the year-to-date, and income and expenses for the past two years, then proceed to enter all the information in one of the credit memo forms included in the CD. The *CRES Solutions* CD provides you with four types of credit memos, depending on the type of loan your client is seeking. The forms are created with all the formulas already built in. A square-boxed header section is provided for each bit of information you must include in a particular first cut, thus if you use the software, you can be sure you haven't missed a single step. All you have to do is enter the correct information and verify that it makes sense. Should you type in the numbers incorrectly the output of the formulas will not fall within reasonable ranges. So if you come up with some unbelievable numbers, double-check your work! In Chapter 7, one of the most commonly used credit memos on the CD is reviewed in detail so you can begin getting some hands-on practice with first cuts, as well as instruction on using the software.

CHAPTER SEVEN

How to Analyze Owner-Occupied Properties

An owner occupied property is a real estate property that is occupied (leased) by the property owner's company or business.

Generally, underwriting owner-occupied commercial real estate consists of two primary elements: (1) real estate value and (2) business value. The lender must analyze both elements in order to avoid taking an undue risk. For example, when analyzing an owner-occupied property, a lender may analyze the value of the real estate based on its ability into generate income under a market rent scenario. This procedure provides insight to the projected value of the real estate and its ability to generate rental income, should it be leased to a tenant other than the owner-occupant. Thus if the owner were to default on the loan and a foreclosure had to take place, the lender can be assured of recouping the loan repayments by renting the property to a third party.

Once a determination of the value and market-rent-income-producing ability of the real estate is made, a lender may then analyze the owner-occupant's business to ascertain whether the business generates sufficient income to service the proposed debt. By doing both analyses, the lender is assured that the debt service can be covered under either scenario.

Analyzing the Real Estate Value

The primary real estate underwriting test for owner-occupied properties includes an analysis of the property's ability to generate income under a market rent scenario—as if the owner-occupant was not the tenant and the space was leased to a nonowner tenant. To complete this analysis, the following must be known:

1. Estimated market rent for the owner-occupied space(s).

2. Typical lease structure for the owner-occupied space(s).

---

3. Average lease term (that is customary for the respective market.)

4. Items paid by lessee (tenant) vs. lessor (landlord).

Where the owner has a lease: In many cases, the owning entity (the entity that owns the real estate) has a lease with the tenant entity (the owning entity's business). This is known as a synthetic lease and is commonly done for tax or accounting purposes. Even if this synthetic lease was written at a market rental rate, you must verify the market rate by examining the market for comparable leases (similar properties that are leased to nonowning tenants.) When you fill out the rent roll form on the CD, the rental income must be "marked-to-market." This means that you must enter the market rent, not the lease rent, in the contract rent field.

Where the owner does not have a separate company owning the real estate, you should recommend that a real estate holding company be created to own the real estate. This good advice will benefit both your client and the lender. From the lender's perspective, a real estate holding company is good because the real estate will not be affected by a problem or failure with the operating business. The property can be sold or leased to another entity even if the owner-operator's business fails. A real estate holding company also benefits the borrower because this structure separates the business owner's property from the business; thus a failure of the operating company does not encumber the property owner's real estate. However, if the occupying business does fail, and as a result the borrower cannot make the mortgage payments, the real estate lender will likely foreclose on the property.

When creating a real estate holding company with a lease to the operating company, the lease should be at market rents and should be for a period of time equal to the term of the loan. Example, if similar properties are leased at $12.00 per square foot per year, with a 3-year lease term, and real estate taxes, insurance, and utilities are included, then you should enter the owner-occupant as a tenant under these lease conditions. This is a projection of how the property would perform if it were leased to a nonowner tenant.

Analyzing the Business Value

To analyze the business, you must know certain basic terms and their meaning. Accordingly, the following are some basic terms used to analyze a small business.

Going Concern Value is the market value of all the tangible and intangible assets of an established business with an indefinite life, if sold in aggregate. Going concern value includes the incremental value associated with the value of the operating business, which is separate from the value of the real estate. However, for certain types of properties (e.g., hotels and motels, restaurants, bowling alleys, marinas, manufacturing enterprises, athletic clubs, landfills, etc.,) the physical real estate assets are integral parts of the ongoing business and should be included in the going concern value.

Investment Value is the specific value of a property to a particular investor or class of investors based on individual investment requirements; distinguished from market value, which is impersonal and detached.

Special Purpose Property is a limited-market property with a unique physical design, special construction materials, or a layout that restricts it from being used by other entities (e.g., churches, museums, schools, clubs, etc.).

To properly package a loan for an owner-occupied property a broker must create a write-up similar to the one we are presenting at the end of this chapter. This write-up will be important regardless of the type of loan or lender you seek.

Lender/Loan Options

One of the largest and most aggressive lenders in the owner-occupied financing world is GE Capital Small Business Finance. They do only full documentation loans up to $15 million. Another major player is an old, well known, and well-funded Wall Street investment banking firm. However, neither of these lenders deals directly with small brokers. As a new commercial broker, you will have to deal with their correspondent lenders—usually banks and large mortgage companies. My company, Coast Investors, is a correspondent to GE and the major Wall Street firm. The write-up presented at the end of this chapter was done for one of these major lenders.

Another option open to the business owner is the Small Business Administration (SBA.) In Chapter 4, I provided you with the basic parameters of an SBA loan. Most mortgage brokers mistakenly believe that SBA loans take a long time. While that may be true of direct SBA loans, it is not true of

SBA guarantee loans. SBA guarantee loans are issued by banks, GE, and other approved SBA lenders, and are partially guaranteed by the SBA. SBA guarantee loans are a viable option when you are working with an owner-occupied business. However, to obtain an SBA guarantee loan, you still have to work with a primary lender like a bank, GE, or the other major Wall Street firm. So learning to create a solid write-up is still important.

Creating a First Cut

The following pages illustrate the steps to create an owner-occupant first cut using the software provided on the *CRES Solutions* CD. Even if you are not using the CD software, you should study this example thoroughly, as it reviews all the elements that you will need to prepare a solid first cut.

First, let's take a look at a few pertinent facts you will need to know in order to begin entering information into the software:

Income/Expense:

When entering income and expenses for an owner-occupied property, enter only the income and expenses that accrue to the real restate; do not include income and expenses related to the business. The goal is to develop a snapshot of the net income the property would produce if it was leased under a market rent scenario. Items related to the business (e.g., gross sales receipts, payroll, health insurance, employee benefits, etc.) should not be included in the real estate analysis.

Common Income items:

- Base rent
- Expense reimbursements (if comparable leases indicate that certain expenses are reimbursed)

Common Expense items:

- Real estate taxes

- Property insurance
- Utilities
- Repairs and Maintenance
- Management fees
- Advertising and marketing
- General and administrative

For New Construction: If the property is being constructed or newly constructed and has no income or expense history, you must estimate the income (based on comparable leases at market rent) and the projected annual expenses. Most property owners will have a schedule of income and expense projections for the project as completed that you can use.

Your project description should include the following information:

- Type of business
- Years in operation
- Profit and Loss statements (for 3 years)
- Balance Sheet
- Summary of Borrower's experience

Once you are prepared with this information, you are ready to create a write-up. The sample credit approval presentation that follows on the next page was prepared using the *CRES Solutions* CD software and demonstrates each required step for an owner occupied property.

Sample Credit Approval Presentation

The example below is for refinancing a 33 room limited service hotel property.

The owner is seeking a $150,000 loan. This presentation contains the key elements you will need to learn to work with owner occupied properties, as well as tips and hints on utilizing the *CRES Solutions* software to its best advantage.

Please note the way this example is set up. The CD contains 4 types of credit memos from which you can select the one most pertinent to your client's needs. Much of the information is already provided for you on the appropriate credit memo form. The credit memo you select will display standard information, and you will then input the specific information required by the data entry fields. Let's take a look:

CREDIT REQUEST

CREDIT APPROVAL PRESENTATION	

PRESENTATION DATE:	11-05-04	PROPOSED LOAN CLOSING DATE:	
BORROWER(S):	Hotel Owner		
CONTACT PERSON:	Mr. Borrower		
SSN / TAX ID NUMBER(S):			
MAILING ADDRESS: CITY: STATE/ZIP:		PHYSICAL ADDRESS: CITY: STATE/ZIP:	

REFERRING BANK: MAILING ADDRESS: CITY: STATE/ZIP:	Coast Investors Capital Group, LLC 2655 Le Jeune RD Suite PH1 Coral Gables FL 33XXX
CONTACT PERSON:	Evald Dupuy
BUSINESS PHONE:	
FAX:	
OTHER PHONE(S):	
CELL PHONE:	
E-MAIL ADDRESS:	

LOAN AMOUNT:	$1,500,000	FORM	1st Mortgage	TYPE:	Conventional

PURPOSE: Refinance limited service hotel located in Ocean Key Florida.

| INTEREST RATE: | ☒ 10 year fixed rate | | FEE: | 1% |
| | Fixed Rate of | | | |

ADJUSTED: Quarterly

| ACCRUAL METHOD: | Actual 360 | AMORTIZATION: | 20 year |
| | | PREPAYMENT PENALTY: | 5.4.3.2.1 |

TERMS: 20 year

REPAYMENT SOURCES:
1. Hotel
2.)
3.)

COLLATERAL:		COST ($)	VALUE
	First position deed to secure debt on all real estate and improvements consisting of a 33 room Limited service hotel located at 3626 Main Street, Mammoth Lakes, Florida.		3,000,000
	☒ All FF&E Attached to Subject R/E ☐ All FF&E Attached & Not Attached to Subject R/E		
			3,000,000
	LOAN to COST and LOAN to VALUE RATIOS:	%	50%

INSURANCE:	AGENT NAME	COMPANY	PHONE

LOAN-TO-VALUE RATIO: (LTV): GUIDELINES:

SELECT ONE OF THE TANGIBLE COLLATERAL TYPES BELOW		
COLLATERAL TYPE	TARGET	MAXIM
☐ Commercial	60%	70%
☒ Hotel/Motel and other Special Use	50%	60%
☐ Improved Commercial Real Estate – All Types Owner	70%	75%
☐ Gas Station/C-Store	50%	55%
☐ Non-owner Occupied	60%	70%

LTV RATIO FOR THIS LOAN: <u>50</u>   **EXCEPTION TO LOAN POLICY:**

GUARANTOR(S):		PHONES	SSN / TIN	F/S DATE	% / $ GTY
NAME ADDRESS CITY/STATE/ZIP E-MAIL					
NAME ADDRESS CITY/STATE/ZIP E-MAIL					
NAME ADDRESS CITY/STATE/ZIP E-MAIL					
NAME ADDRESS CITY/STATE/ZIP E-MAIL					

Mr. Borrower is requesting a 10-year, fixed loan converting to a 30-day LIBOR + 400 basis point after the 10-year period to purchase the above described property.

SOURCES AND USES OF FUNDS

Input your borrower's specific information in the chart on the following page.

USES OF FUNDS	Who/Explanation			
Purchase Land		#DIV/0!	$0	
Purchase Land & Building		#DIV/0!	$0	
Construction		#DIV/0!	$0	
Interim Interest		#DIV/0!	$0	
Contingency		#DIV/0!	$0	
Equipment		#DIV/0!	$0	
Refinance Existing Debt		#DIV/0!	$1,500,000	
Refinance Existing Debt		#DIV/0!	$0	
Refinance Existing Debt		#DIV/0!	$0	
Refinance Existing Debt		#DIV/0!	$0	
Refinance Existing Debt		#DIV/0!	$0	
Working Capital		#DIV/0!	$0	
Other		#DIV/0!	$0	
Closing Costs		#DIV/0!	$0	
Total Uses		#DIV/0!	**$0**	
SOURCES OF FUNDS				
Bank - GE		#DIV/0!	$0	
SBA 7a		#DIV/0!	$0	
SBA 504 (Net Debenture)		#DIV/0!	$0	
Other		#DIV/0!	$0	
Seller Note		#DIV/0!	$0	
Equity		#DIV/0!	$0	
Total Sources		#DIV/0!	**$0**	

FULL COLLATERAL DESCRIPTION and VALUATION/ANALYSIS

The collateral for this transaction will be a first position deed to secure debt on all real estate and improvements consisting of a 50-room limited service hotel located in the resort town of Ocean Key, Florida, with an approximate value of $4,000,000. Included in the collateral is a UCC filing first lien on all machinery, equipment, furniture, and fixtures now owned and hereafter acquired.

STRENGTHS & WEAKNESSES

STRENGTHS: Describe as best you can the community, the property, and why the property is showing the income it is showing and what the future projected income is proposed to be and why.

• The property is located in the resort town of Ocean Key Florida, a fast-growing Florida east coast resort town. Condominium development is in full force and associated service industries are growing to meet the increasing demand. The property shows excellent debt service coverage.

WEAKNESSES:

Property is 25–30 years old. There are 5 other hotels in town.

COMPANY HISTORY

MANAGEMENT

If you are creating this for an investor property then enter the real estate management history of the buyer. If he has no previous real estate experience, enter a detailed background and resume of the individual.

If the property being analyzed is an owner-occupied property, then enter the management experience of the borrower as it relates to his business.

INDUSTRY/COMPETITION

Be explicit with competition. Don't say we do not have competition because we are a unique property. All properties and business have competition.

FINANCIAL ANALYSIS

Fiscal year end and interim financial statement.

Income Statement:

Net income increased (decreased) approximately x% in 2003 and is on track for a larger increase in 2004. 2004 revenue is up approximately 10% when annualized for the year. Revenue has remained consistent over the last three years. The numbers should come in even stronger for 2004 due to the early opening of the mountain for snow skiing. The company shows EBITA of approximately $260M for 2002, $255M for 2003 and $177M for the seven months ended July 31, 2004.

Liquidity:

Mr. Borrower has substantial liquidity available in savings if the need arises. (Liquidity of a borrower is very important in hotel financing or in any other investor property financing because in case of higher vacancies the borrower can access private funds.)

Leverage:

Cash Flow & Debt Service: The operating concern demonstrates the ability to service the proposed debt in 2002, 2003, and 2004 with DCR of 2.02, 1.99, and 2.36 respectively (including a $36,000 salary for owners).

Once you have entered the information required, this chart provides you with a solid DSCR upon which the lender can rely.

In $000's				
Type of Statement	Tax Rtn	Tax Rtn	Tax Rtn	Co Prep
Date	12/31/2001	12/31/2002	12/31/2003	7/31/2004
# Months	4	12	12	7
Revenues	$218,667	$714,679	$716,759	$425,280
Net Before Tax	-$32,788	$140,280	$150,020	$120,259
Depreciation	$15,100	$34,093	$30,925	
Amortization				
Interest - Loans	$38,729	$85,209	$74,242	$56,878
Rents				
Other				
Net Cash Before Debt Service	**$21,041**	**$259,582**	**$255,187**	**$177,137**
Bank - GE	$42,848	$128,543	$128,543	$74,984
SBA 504				
Other	$0	$0	$0	
Total Debt Service	**$42,848**	**$128,543**	**$128,543**	**$74,984**
Cash After Debt Service	-$21,807	$131,039	$126,644	$102,153
Coverage	0.49	2.02	1.99	2.36

DEBT Detail as of Date

Lender	Amount/Bal	Balance	PMT	Rate	Maturity	Amor	Collateral
Bank - GE	$1,500,000		$128,543	5.96%	Jul-24	20	1st Lien: Real Estate
Other	$0	$0	$0				
Total Proposed	$1,500,000	$0	$128,543				
Other	$0	$0	$0				
Total Existing	$0	$0	$0				
Total Prop & Exist	$1,500,000	$0	$128,543				

Analysis of Accounts Receivable & Accounts Payable:

As of July 31, 2004. This is a hotel and A/P and A/R are paid in 30 days.

Accounts Receivable:

None listed

Accounts Payable:

None listed

GUARANTOR(S)

Mr. Borrower's personal financial statement shows a net worth of $5,387,000. Assets are centered in real estate, which includes the limited service. Mr. Borrower also has a 33% ownership of a 40-room hotel located in Ocean Key, Florida, and a 42% ownership of a 120-room Super Hotel. In addition, he has $250,000 in savings. Liabilities consist of real estate mortgages.

CRITICAL ISSUES

None

SUBJECT TO & ADDITIONAL REQUIREMENTS:

1. Satisfactory review of current appraisal report indicating a minimum value of $___

2. Max LTV of _____%

3. Satisfactory review of survey (if required by title company for endorsements)

4. Satisfactory review of title commitment

5. Proof of insurance (and flood insurance if in flood zone)

6. Proof of cash injection of _____

7. Satisfactory review of Phase I Environmental Report

8. Satisfactory review of TSA Report

9. Satisfactory review of supplemental Asbestos Report

10. Satisfactory review of supplemental lead based paint report

11. Subordination Agreement from _____

_____

12. Copy of SBA Authorization for 504 loan or 7a loan

13. Satisfactory review of lease agreements

14. Copy of commitment letter from _____

15. showing 2nd DOT position behind Bank with
a minimum loan term of _____ yrs

16. Copy of executed purchase contract

17. Proof of completion of improvements to property_____

18. Detailed breakdown of construction costs; Proof of pay off of loan from

_____

As you can see, the *CRES Solutions* software will generate a comprehensive first cut package that allows the lender to overview all pertinent aspects of the transaction at a glance. Your job is to collect and enter all pertinent information into the appropriate credit memo. If you've used the rent roll calculator demonstrated in Chapter 6, much of this information will already be at your fingertips when you sit down to prepare the write-up.

Study this example, and refer back to it frequently as you review the underwriting guidelines provided in previous and subsequent chapters.

Chapter Eight

Stated Income/Stated Asset Programs

Stated small business real estate loans virtually eliminate the obstacles that have made small commercial mortgage brokering difficult and time consuming in the past. These relatively new loans are available up to $2,000,000 for qualified borrowers.

Stated income/stated asset programs are driven by the credit worthiness and financial strength of the borrower. In these programs the borrower is asked to fill out and sign a form containing a number of questions—two of the questions relate to the average yearly income and net worth of the borrower and co-borrower. This form has to be signed by the borrower and coborrower. In the case of the multifamily program a rent roll form is also required to be filled out and signed. The rent roll form asks for the actual rent on each apartment as well as the market rent (the rental rate at which a similar apartment is renting in the market). When these documents are submitted, a conditional letter of intent can be issued by the lender and signed by the borrower. Finally, an appraisal is ordered. The appraisal must confirm the statements made in the rent roll, assigning a value to the property that supports the requested loan amount. If the information provided is certified accurate by the appraiser, the loan is closed.

What makes these new programs so attractive is that the loan is driven solely by quality of credit, quality of collateral, and collateral cash flow. Stated income/ stated asset loan programs cut through much of the red tape involved with full documentation loans. You do not have to worry about loan committees or hard equity financing. There is no need for the borrower to produce documents such as tax returns, financial statements, IRS form 4506 (verification of tax filing), seasoned closing funds, or asset and income statements. Once the application is complete, prequalification can be determined in as little as 72 hours.

The following is a list of typical guidelines for these types of Alt-A (Stated) commercial mortgage programs.

Alt-A (Stated) Commercial Mortgage Underwriting Profile

• Stating the income and assets of the borrower.

• Stated debt service coverage ratio.

• Small-balance mortgages, i.e., $150,000 to $5,000,000.

• As high as 90 percent LTV on commercial with 7000 credit scores and 85 percent on multifamily.

• Par and par-plus pricing.

• 25-year terms with no balloons on commercial, 30 year terms on multifamily.

• Fixed and adjustable rates.

• Purchase, rate and term, and cash-out refinances.

• Minimum 660 FICO score.

Credit Criteria	Alt A (stated income) (1)	Alt A Express (stated income)
Minimum Loan Size	$100,000	$100,000
Maximum Loan Size	$1,000,000 ($1,500,000 for SBA 504 loans)	$500,000
Minimum Individual Guaranty %	Each >= 50% & >=50% of EPC & OC	Each >= 50% & >=50% of EPC & OC
Target Owner Occupancy	>= 25%	> 50%
Bankruptcy	3 years min.	3 years min.
Foreclosure	5 years min.	5 years min.

The following table defines the credit strength required by the borrower in order to obtain various loans. You will note that because of the simplicity of stated loans, a higher credit score is required to obtain one.

Credit Criteria	Alt A (stated income) (1)	Alt A Express (stated income)
Minimum Loan Size Maximum Loan Size	$100,000 $1,000,000 ($1,500,000 for SBA 504 loans)	$100,000 $500,000
Minimum Individual Guaranty % Target Owner Occupancy	Each >= 50% & >=50% of EPC & OC >= 25%	Each >= 50% & >=50% of EPC & OC > 50%
Bankruptcy Foreclosure	3 years min. 5 years min.	3 years min. 5 years min.

Program	Transaction Type	Minimum Average FICO	Maximum LTV – 1st TD	Maximum CLTV
Alt A Express (stated income)	Purchase	700 690 680 670	90% 85% 80% 75%	90%
	Purchase or Rate/Term Refinance	660	70%	
Investor	Purchase	680	75%	80%
	Rate/Term Refinance	660	70%	75%
	Cash Out Refinance	660	65%	70%

In the owner occupied stated income program, borrowers complete a 5 page stated income application. The subject property must have a minimum Debt Service Coverage (DSCR) of 1:1 Net Operating Income (NOI) based on current leases, expenses, and market conditions, as verified with an appraisal.

The owner must demonstrate occupancy of at least 25% or minimum DSCR of 1.25:1 (NOI) based on current leases, expenses, and market conditions, and verified with an appraisal.

Average FICO of all guarantors/borrowers should be greater to or equal than the minimum average FICO indicated in the above table. If using a tri-merge credit report, the middle scores are used in the calculation. If two FICOs are generated, the lower score is used in the calculation.

CLTV is the LTV of all liens against the property, including 1st TD, 2nd TD, and seller financing, divided by the appraised value or acquisition cost. Borrower must have 10% equity injection for most transactions.

This is a comparison table of the three programs offered by Coast Investors: full documentation, stated and investors.

Collateral Eligibility	Full Doc	Alt-A/ Alt-A Express	Investor
Office	YES	YES	YES
Office/Warehouse	YES	YES	YES
Medical/Dental Office	YES	YES	YES
Office Condo	YES	YES	YES
Retail	YES	YES	YES
Mixed Use Commercially Zoned	YES	YES	YES
Auto Repair (Phase I)	YES	YES	YES
Contractor Yard (Phase I)	YES	YES	YES
Dry Cleaners (Phase I)	YES	YES	YES
Day Care / Vocational School	YES	NO	NO

As you can see, the Alt-A stated product is available in all collateral categories. The only limitation is a borrower maximum of $1,000,000. There are a few other things to keep in mind with the Alt-A products. Mixed use properties are subject to restrictions depending on the state. The borrower should not be residing at the subject property. All subject collateral must be in average or better condition, confirmed by the appraisal, and must have a remaining economic life at least equal to the term of the proposed loan.

Again, the main difference between full documentation loans and stated income loans is the time it takes to obtain a conditional letter of intent (CLI). With a stated program a borrower can have a CLI in 48 hours. This letter spells out the terms and conditions under which the lender will close the proposed loan. If the borrower is in agreement with the terms presented, the borrower knows that he has a loan and can proceed with the purchase or refinance of his property without delay.

Initiating Your Commercial Loan Process

The stated loans covered in this chapter require a shorter (5-page) loan application than do full documentation loans. For full documentation loans you should start with the loan application, preferably one provided by the lender or lenders to whom you propose to send the deal. If you do not have any lender relationships established yet, use the application found on the *CRES Solutions* CD. Some small loan lenders still want to use the residential loan application even though it is for residential loans. In any case, once the loan application is complete, you should proceed to write up the property using one of the templates provided in the CD. For the stated loans we have discussed in this chapter, the write-up should contain the following information:

Express Multifamily Stated Guidelines

Required documentation: Signed 1003 residential application, tri-merge credit report, special rent roll signed by all appropriate parties, current operating and year-to-date statement signed, REO schedule for conditional approval letter.

In this program **NO PDRs, NO TAX RETURNS, NO VOEs.**

One of the key requirements of all commercial stated programs is the submission of **digital photos** of property and street scenes with the application.

Asset Quality: Average or better. No significant deferred maintenance. No mixed use property under this program.

Third Party Deposit: When a conditional commitment letter is received, a check for $2,500 to pay for appraisal, environmental and any other third party reports is required from the borrower. Other cost: $500 (Include loan doc's, U/W., etc.) to 15 units, $1,000 for 16 to 30 units, $1,500 for 30+ units (50 Units Max.)

Sizing: Start rate, appraisal NOI.

Post Close Liquidity: The owner must have post closing cash of at least 5% of the loan amount.

Net Worth: The owner must have a net worth equal to or greater than the loan amount.

Experience: Borrowers must have current or recent income property ownership in the area. Experience is always a plus in all real estate transactions.

Recourse: Full. The borrower must sign personally for the loan.

SMSA: The minimum population of the town where the property is located has to be at least 25,000 and be stabilized, not declining.

Impounds: The lender will hold a required escrow for taxes and insurance.

Borrowers: Individuals, revocable trusts, maximum 2-member LLC (no sub entities). (In Florida, must be trust or LLC.) I recommend that you always structure the transactions with a corporate structure.

Rate Caps: The interest rate charge cannot change more than 3% maximum first adjustment/1% subsequent/6% lifetime.

This express program is quick and easy. A closing can be scheduled in less than 30 days. Usual delays are due to not receiving required documentation.

Stated Multifamily Guidelines

Quality: "A" and "B"—average and above properties (minor deferred maintenance considered.) No mixed use considered.

Sizing: 6 Mo ARM: Size/qual @ 5.50% or fully indexed rate 3-10 Yr. Hybrid: size/qual @ start rate.

Seasoning: 1-12 months—Refinances generally not considered during first 12 months. 12-24 months—Refinances generally considered up to 90% of original purchase price.

Credit: Minimum 700 middle credit score on primary guarantor. No mortgage derogatories within previous 36 months.

Strong financial sponsorship required, meaning that the buyer or owner has to have a significant net worth with liquidity.

Rate Caps: 6 mo. ARM: 1% every 6 months, 6% lifetime over start rate (10% minimum). 3-10 hybrids: 3% first adjustment, 1% subsequent, 6% lifetime over start rate.

Recourse: Full. Nonrecourse with standard carve-outs considered at lower LTV. Call first.

Impounds: Taxes and insurance typically required.

Reports: $2,500 deposit typically required for appraisal, environmental, and property inspection on loans up to $3 million. $3,950 deposit required for loans from $3 to $5 million.

Appraisal fee deposit may be higher on larger loan amounts/units/remote location.

Ancillary Costs: $1,375 up to $1 million, $1,475 up to $3 million, $1,575 over $3 million for U/W, admin and docs, plus $150 legal review/entity. Additional doc fees as required based on entity structure, post closing requirements (holdbacks, side letter agreements, super-rush, re-U/W, re-lock fee.)

Rate Locks: Most programs at time of approval or 60 day advance rate lock after conditional approval with nonrefundable $250 fee.

All Programs: Credit file must be received within 21 days of rate lock or the lock is subject to cancellation.

Assumability: One time with 1% fee and approval.

Price Adjustments: If middle credit score is less than 660, please send copy of credit report with new loan submission. Minimum 25% mixed use property; maximum income from commercial use. Seasoning exceptions on refinances.

No more than 50% singles in project. Any additional creates perceived risk.

Risk based pricing: All loans are subject to adjustment for age and property condition, unstable historical operations, multi-ayered borrowing structures, credit scores, subsidized housing, high percentage of singles, and other exceptions to the underwriting guidelines.

Lending Institution fees

Various lending institutions have different fee schedules for commercial loan applications and processing. The range of fees varies widely amongst these institutions. Your loan officer will be happy to provide more information on the schedule of fees for each institution. A range of potential fees for several leading institutions follows:

Attorney: $0 - $5,000

Underwriting: 0 - $2,000

Appraisal: $0 - $3,000

Opinion letters for nonrecourse loans: $500 - $750

Note: some lenders may charge higher fees

Chapter Nine

Common Practices for Underwriting Commercial Properties

Now that we have reviewed the underwriting guidelines for multifamily (apartment) and owner-occupied properties, emphasizing the stated basis, we will devote our attention to underwriting guidelines for full documentation loans. This chapter provides you an overview of commercial property underwriting guidelines for full documentation loans. The following chapters will provide you a detailed look at an underwriter's expectations for each of the various types of commercial properties.

Please keep in mind that each lender has different views of underwriting, and therefore this chapter should be utilized as a guideline only. The following underwriting practices were compiled to provide the broker with a list of factors that can affect the underwriting for commercial properties. What follows will allow you to do a first cut underwriting analysis.

Commercial Property Types	
Office	Central Business District (CBD) Office Suburban Garden Office Suburban High Rise Medical Office Other Office

Commercial Property Types	
Retail	Grocery Anchored Retail
	Other Anchored Retail
	Free Standing Retail
	Strip Center – Anchored
	Strip Center – Unanchored
	Mall – Super Regional
	Mall – Regional
	Specialty Center
	Unanchored Retail
	Single Tenant Investment (Credit Tenant Lease)
	Single Tenant Non-Investment
	Outlet Center
	Other Retail
Industrial	Warehouse (Single-or Multi Tenant)
	Manufacturing
	Research & Development
	Flex Space
	Light Industrial
	Heavy Industrial
	Other Industrial
Multifamily	Low-Rise Garden Apartments
	Mid-Rise Apartments
	Student Housing
	Military Housing
	Townhouse Style
	Co-op
	Other Apartments
	Mobile Home Park MHP 1 Star
	MHP 2 Star
	MHP 3 Star
	MHP 4 Star
	MHP 5 Star

Commercial Property Types	
Healthcare	Nursing Home Congregate Care Assisted Living Other Healthcare
Hotel / Motel	Full Service – Luxury Full Service – Resort Full Service – Mid-scale Limited Service – Mid-scale Limited Service – Economy Limited Service- Extended Stay
Self Storage Mini-Storage	Climate Controlled Other Self Storage

General Market and Location Characteristics

Most lenders look for established or emerging markets with a population of at least 50,000 with no population declines since 1980 based on US Census data. In-fill locations that are reasonably insulated from the threat of new supply are preferred. Property must be located near, and easily accessible to, major highways/freeways, employment sources, and other demand generators. The economic and employment base of the area should be diverse.

Property Condition and Characteristics

In commercial financing, a property less than 15 years old is preferred. Older properties in good condition and having undergone material renovations within the last ten years are also acceptable. If a borrower is seeking a 25-year loan, the remaining useful life of the property must be at least that many years. The remaining useful life of a property is typically addressed in the appraisal of the property.

Building design, floor plan, technological capabilities, and amenities have to be appropriate for the immediate market area. Accordingly, multiuse properties are more desirable to a lender than a single-use property. A multiuse property is a building that can be converted from a given use by one owner and easily changed to another use by another owner.

A building in good condition is more desirable to a long-term lender than a building that requires significant repairs after purchase. In this case it is best to have the seller make the repairs as part of the sale transaction. Alternatively, the prospective buyer/borrower could secure a rehab loan (rehabilitation construction loan) to do the repairs, and once the repairs are dealt with, he or she can convert to a term loan.

Operating Performance

If the property being purchased is an investor property, the property should show strong historical operating performance with no material declines in revenue or NOI over the past two years.

The property's occupancy should be at or above the local market's average occupancy with no material declines over the past two years; however, newly constructed or recently rehabilitated properties that have not reached stabilized occupancy are considered by most lenders.

The tenant base of an investor property should be diverse and creditworthy, and the borrower and property manager should have significant experience in owning and managing, respectively, several properties similar to the mortgaged property and situated in comparable markets.

During due diligence of the property for loan purposes, the underwriter will require documentation proving compliance with the law:

- Zoning compliance letter.
- Certificates of occupancy.
- Applicable licenses and permits.
- Borrower disclosure regarding current litigation.

Either the borrower or the borrower's outside legal counsel must provide written certification of compliance with applicable statutes, including: parking rules and regulations, zoning, land use, occupancy, environmental protection, access and egress, facilities for disabled persons, equal opportunity, fair housing, and antidiscrimination.

Where a property does not conform with current laws or regulations relating to use, size, density, or parking, satisfactory evidence should be obtained of legislation, building codes, or local zoning variances that permit the improvements to be rebuilt to predamage use, size, and density in the event that less than 50% of the improvements are destroyed. Such evidence may include legal opinions and/or letters from the land use jurisdiction. Law and ordinance insurance on these properties might be required.

Knowledge of any illegal activities on the mortgaged property, including activities relating to controlled substances, should be disclosed.

Easements

Standard utility easements providing service to the mortgaged property are acceptable if they (1) are noted on the survey, (2) are properly accepted to the title insurance policy, and (3) do not encroach upon the improvements.

Generally, a property is not acceptable if it shares or is burdened by (1) primary ingress or egress through an easement or private road, or (2) on-site or off-site recreational facilities or amenities that are not under the exclusive control of the borrower.

Ground Leases

If the mortgage loan is to be secured in whole or in part by a ground lease of the mortgaged property, the ground lease will meet the ground lease requirements. Unless the ground lease payments are required to be made on a monthly basis, the borrower might be required to establish an escrow account for such payments.

Documentation Checklist for Full Documentation Loans

The following items are commonly required for each mortgage loan:

Proposed Loan Documentation

Promissory note

Mortgage or deed of trust

Assignment of leases and rents

Assignment of management agreement (if applicable)

UCC-I financing statements (encumbering all fixtures, appliances, etc.)

Environmental indemnity agreement (insurance)

Guaranty agreement

Lead-based paint acknowledgment and indemnification agreement

Asbestos 0 & M Agreement (if applicable)

Other Documentation

Copy of title policy

Mortgage title insurance commitment

Evidence of required insurance and special endorsements (if applicable)

Copies of all recorded exception documents

UCC financing statement search, tax lien search and judgment search

Real property tax search

Copies of most recent real property tax bills

Municipal department violation searches,
including environmental lien searches

Leases

Copies of all leases, including all modifications and
amendments (commercial tenants only)

Copies of standard form lease (commercial and multifamily)

Rent Roll and Occupancy Statements;

Estoppel Letters and Subordination Agreements;

Estoppel letters executed by all space tenants (commercial tenants only)

Subordination, nondisturbance and Attornment agreements (commercial tenants only)

Zoning, Use and Occupancy

Copies of certificate of occupancy/building permit

Letter from municipality (zoning and building compliance)

Zoning comfort letter

Copy of management agreement

Survey

Casualty insurance documentation

Copy of all risk insurance policy (hazard & liability)

Boiler damage and liability policy (if applicable)

Flood insurance policy or evidence that premises are not in flood zone

Evidence of payment of one year's insurance premium

Law and ordinance coverage if property is non-conforming.

Borrower Organizational Documents

Where borrower is corporation or corporate general partner:

Articles of Incorporation and all amendments thereto, certified by Secretary of State where incorporated;

Copy of bylaws, certified by borrower

Certificate of good standing issued by secretary of state (or equivalent) of state where incorporated

Borrowing resolution of board of directors;

Incumbency and secretary certificate

Where Borrower is Limited or General Partner of a Partnership:

Articles of incorporation of general partnership and all amendments thereto, certified by secretary of state where incorporated; certificate of good standing of general partner

Copy of limited partnership agreement

Certificate of limited partnership and all amendments thereto, certified by appropriate office

Evidence of publication of certificate of limited partnership (if required)

Borrowing resolution

Where Borrower is Limited Liability Company:

Articles of incorporation and all amendments thereto, certified as filed by the secretary of state where organized

Copy of operating agreement, certified by borrower

Certificate of good standing;

Borrowing resolution of members/manager.Simply by reviewing this list you will better understand the benefit of stated basis loans, particularly when time is of the essence. Compare the checklist above with the documentation checklist provided in Chapter 8 for stated loans. Being aware of all your options will enable you to provide the best possible service to your clients.

CHAPTER TEN

Office Properties Underwriting Guidlines

Underwriting Profile

In order to obtain funding, an office loan package should reflect the following key characteristics.

Central Business District (CBD) Office

- Max. LTV–80%.

- Max. amortization – 15 to 20 years.

- Min. DSCR - 1.25x.

- Min. vacancy reserve – the greater of actual or market vacancy, typically 7% to 10%.

- Min. tenant improvement and leasing commission cost (TI/LC)–the greater of actual or $1.00 per square foot.

- Min. replacement reserves–the greater of actual or $0.18 to $0.20 per square foot.

- Capitalization rate–use market-driven capitalization rate; typically 8% to 11%.

Suburban Garden Office

- Max. LTV–80%.

- Max. amortization – 25 to 30 years.

- Min. DSCR - 1.25x.

- Min. vacancy reserve–the greater of actual or

market vacancy; typically 7% to 10%.

• Min. tenant improvement and leasing commission cost (TI/LC)–the greater of actual or $1.00 per square foot.

• Min. replacement reserves–the greater of actual or $0.18 to $0.20 per square foot.

• Capitalization rate–use market-driven capitalization rate; typically 9% to 11%.

Suburban High Rise

• Max. LTV - 80%.

• Max. amortization – 25 to 30 years.

• Min. DSCR–1.25x.

• Min. vacancy reserve – the greater of actual or market vacancy; typically 7% to 10%.

• Min. tenant improvement and leasing commission cost (TI/LC)–the greater of actual or $1.00 per square foot.

• Min. replacement reserves–the greater of actual or $0.18 to $0.20 per square foot.

• Capitalization rate–use market-driven capitalization rate; typically 8% to 11%.

Medical Office

• Max. LTV–80%.

• Max. amortization–25 to 30 years.

• Min. DSCR–1.25x.

• Min. vacancy reserve–the greater of actual or market vacancy; typically 7% to 10%.

• Min. tenant improvement and leasing commission cost (TI/LC)–the greater of actual or $1.00 per square foot.

• Min. replacement reserves–the greater of actual or $0.18 to $0.20 per square foot.

- Capitalization rate–use market-driven capitalization rate; typically 8% to 11%.

Other Office

- Max. LTV - 80%.

- Max. amortization–25 to 30 years.

- Min. DSCR–1.25x.

- Min. vacancy reserve–the greater of actual or market vacancy; typically 7% to 10%.

- Min. tenant improvement and leasing commission cost (TI/LC)–the greater of actual or $1.00 per square foot.

- Min. replacement reserves–the greater of actual or $0.18 to $0.20 per square foot.

Capitalization rate–use market-driven capitalization rate; typically 8% to 11%.

Class A Single Tenant

- Max. LTV - 80%–credit of tenant required.

- Max. amortization–25 to 30 years, the term should exceed the term of the mortgage by three to five years.

- Min. DSCR–1.25x.

- Min. vacancy reserve–the greater of actual or market vacancy; typically 7% to 10%.

- Min. tenant improvement and leasing commission cost (TI/LC)–the greater of actual or $1.00 per square foot.

- Min. replacement reserves–the greater of actual or $0.18 to $0.20 per square foot.

- Capitalization rate–use market-driven capitalization rate, typically 8% to 11%.

General Guidelines

Market and Location

The property should be located on or near a main thoroughfare and easily accessible to pedestrians as well as to vehicular traffic.

The property should be located in a neighborhood well-lighted in the evening with adequate food/restaurants and retail facilities within close proximity (linkage factors).

Property Condition and Characteristics

The property should have a minimum of two elevators for buildings over three stories and at least four elevators for buildings over 12 stories.

The property should have a minimum parking ratio of 4.0 spaces per 1,000 square feet of net rental area for suburban locations; CBD locations will be evaluated relative to local market ratios.

Property Operating Performance

The operating performance should illustrate a minimum occupancy of 85%.

Full service (Triple-net, NNN) or pro-rata share of insurance, taxes, and common area maintenance expenses are typically passed through to the tenants; this should be illustrated as both an expense and an offsetting tenant reimbursement.

Lease expirations that account for more than 25% of total leases square footage or total revenue in any given year may require a debt service reserve to mitigate the rollover risk.

Properties in which owner-occupied or owner-affiliated tenants occupy more than 20% of total revenue may require a higher interest rate spread.

Normalizing Income and Expense Considerations

Calculate potential gross income (PGI) by adding the annual in-place revenue generated by the current tenants plus the annual income generated from vacant space at market rent. Then apply the appropriate vacancy reserve to calculate effective gross income.

Adjustments to the income may include:

Mark to market any rents from leases that are written above or below market rent (e.g., if a tenant pays $10.00/SF and the market rent for comparable properties is $8.00, consider adjusting the rental income to $8.00/SF).

Consider subtracting any rental income from any tenant who is 60 days or more delinquent.

Include percentage rent, expense reimbursement, and other income (e.g., parking fees, vending, storage fees, and ancillary services).

Adjustments to the expenses may include:

Increasing, decreasing, or normalizing the underwritten expenses based upon historical expense trends.

Apply the greater of the actual or market management fee whether the property is professionally managed or owner-managed, typically 3% to 5%.

Consider applying an expense growth rate of 3% to represent escalation of expenses for the next 12 months. Remove any insurance expense that is not specifically related to the real estate.

Remove any nonrecurring expenses from the underwritten expenses. Reallocate any capital expenses from repairs and maintenance to capital expenditures.

Consider applying a TI/LC reserve if the annual debt service coverage falls below 1.10 (TI/LC Stress DSCR) throughout the loan term.

CHAPTER ELEVEN

Retail Underwriting Guidelines

Underwriting Profile

Anchored Retail (with national tenant as anchor)

Includes grocery anchored retail, other anchored retail, strip center–anchored, mall, super regional, mall–regional, specialty center, other retail

- Max. LTV–75% to 80%.

- Max. amortization – 25 to 30 years.

- Min. DSCR – 1.25x.

- Min. vacancy reserve – the greater of actual or market vacancy; typically 7% to 10%.

- Min. tenant improvement and leasing commission cost (TI/LC) – the greater of actual or $0.70 per square foot.

- Min. replacement reserves – the greater of actual or $0.15 to $0.20 per square foot.

- Capitalization rate – use market-driven capitalization rate, typically 9% to 11%.

Unanchored Retail (complimentary tenant mix)

Includes unanchored retail, strip center—unanchored, single tenant non-investment, outlet center, other retail

- Max. LTV – 75% to 80%.

- Max. amortization – 25 to 30 years.

- Min. DSCR – 1.25x.

- Min. vacancy reserve – the greater of actual or market vacancy; typically 7% to 10%.

- Min. tenant improvement and leasing commission cost (TI/LC) – the greater of actual or $0.75 per square foot.

- Min. replacement reserves – the greater of actual or $0.15 to $0.20 per square foot.

- Capitalization rate – use market-driven capitalization rate, typically 9% to 11%.

Freestanding Retail (should be a credit tenant with sales history)

- Max. LTV – 75% to 80%.

- Max. amortization – 20 to 30 years (lease should extend 5 years beyond the loan term).

- Min. DSCR – 1.40x.

- Min. vacancy reserve – the greater of actual or market vacancy; typically 7% to 10%.

- Min. tenant improvement and leasing commission cost (TI/LC) – the greater of actual or $0.75 per square foot.

- Min. replacement reserves – the greater of actual or $0.15 to $0.20 per square foot.

- Capitalization rate – use market-driven capitalization rate; typically 9% to 11%.

Single Tenant Investment (Credit Tenant Lease)

Tenant should be rated "investment grade" and have revenues of $25,000,000 and a net worth of $5,000,000.

- Max. LTV – up to 100%.

- Max. amortization – 20 to 30 years (lease should extend 5 years beyond the loan term).

• Min. DSCR – 1.000x to 1.003x.

• Min. vacancy reserve – typically 0% to 3%.

• Min. tenant improvement and leasing Commission Cost (TI/LC) – typically zero.

• Min. replacement reserves – the greater of actual or $0.15 to $0.20 per square foot.

• Capitalization rate – use market-driven capitalization rate, typically 7% to 9%.

General Guidelines

Market and Location

The property should have good visual exposure from adjacent streets and/or major freeways/highways.

Property Condition and Characteristics

The property should be configured for truck ingress, egress, accessibility, and minimization of traffic flow congestion.

Store frontage, depth, and overall size should be appropriate for the market.

Second story retail is commonly discounted unless long-term, strong tenancy, and quantifiable market information is used to support.

Minimum parking ratio of 4.0 spaces per 1,000 SF net rental area. Higher parking ratios may be required for tenants with higher parking demands such as restaurants, theaters, and grocery stores.

Normalizing Income and Expense Considerations

Calculate potential gross income (PGI) by adding the annual in-place revenue generated by the current tenants to the annual income generated from vacant space at market rent. Then apply the appropriate vacancy reserve to calculate effective gross income.

Adjustments to the income may include:

Mark to market any rents from leases that are written above or below market rent (e.g., if a tenant pays $10.00/SF and the market rent for comparable properties is $8.00, consider adjusting the rental income to $8.00/SF).

Consider subtracting any rental income from any tenant who is 60 days or more delinquent.

Include percentage rent, expense reimbursement, and other income (e.g., parking fees, vending, storage fees, and ancillary services). With percentage rent, use a 2- or 3-year average of historical percentage rental income attributable to each tenant; note any fluctuations in sales revenues and compare to other regional stores' sales.

Typical adjustments to the expenses:

Increasing, decreasing, or normalizing the underwritten expenses based upon historical expense trends.

Apply the greater of the actual or market management fee whether the property is professionally managed or owner-managed, typically 3% to 5%.

Consider applying an expense growth rate of 3% to represent escalation of expenses for the next 12 months. Remove any insurance expense that is not specifically related to the real estate.

Remove any nonrecurring expenses from the underwritten expenses. Reallocate any capital expenses from repairs and maintenance to capital expenditures.

Consider applying a TI/LC reserve if the annual debt service coverage falls below 1.10 (TI/LC Stress DSCR) throughout the loan term.

CHAPTER TWELVE

Industrial Underwriting Guidelines

Underwriting Profile

Includes warehouse (Single or Multi tenant), manufacturing, research and development, flex space, light industrial, heavy industrial, other industrial

- Max. LTV – 75% to 80%.

- Max. amortization – 25 years.

- Min. DSCR – 1.20 to 1.25x.

- Min. vacancy reserve – the greater of actual or market vacancy, typically 7% to 10%.

- Min. tenant improvement and leasing commission cost (TI/LC) – the greater of actual or $0.25 to $0.35 per square foot.

- Min. replacement reserves – the greater of actual or $0.10 to $0.20 per square foot.

- Capitalization rate – use market-driven capitalization rate, typically 7% to 11%.

General Guidelines

Property Condition and Characteristics

Should have configuration for truck turnaround, ingress, egress, accessibility, and minimization of traffic flow congestion.

Warehouse ceiling heights should be adequate to accommodate forklifts and palettes.

Normalizing Income and Expense Considerations

Calculate potential gross income (PGI) by adding the annual in-place revenue generated by the current tenants plus the annual income generated from vacant space at market rent. Then apply the appropriate vacancy reserve to calculate effective gross income.

Adjustments to the income may include:

Mark to market any rents from leases that are written above or below market rent. For example, if a tenant pays $4.00/SF and the market rent for comparable properties is $3.00, consider adjusting the rental income to $3.00/SF.

Consider subtracting any rental income from any tenant who is 60 days or more delinquent.

Include expense reimbursements, CAM, and other income (e.g., yard storage, parking fees, and ancillary services).

Typical adjustments to the expenses include:

Increasing, decreasing, or normalizing the underwritten expenses based upon historical expense trends.

Apply the greater of the actual or market management fee whether the property is professionally managed or owner-managed, typically 2% to 4%.

Consider applying an expense growth rate of 3% to represent escalation of expenses for the next 12 months.

Remove any insurance expense that is not specifically related to the real estate.

Remove any nonrecurring expenses from the underwritten expenses.

Reallocate any capital expenses from repairs and maintenance to capital expenditures.

Consider applying a TI/LC reserve if the annual debt service coverage falls below 1.10 (TI/LC Stress DSCR) throughout the loan term.

The Art of Commercial Mortgage Brokering

CHAPTER THIRTEEN

Hotel/Motel Underwriting Guidelines

Underwriting Profile

Hotel financing is a specialty niche better left to the very knowledgeable. The investors in this market, like GE capital, are very large and financially choosy companies. GE finances only limited service hotels, as you will note below.

Full Service Hotels

Includes full service —luxury, full service—resort, full service—midscale (e.g., Hilton, Marriott, Holiday Inn, etc.). Caters primarily to business, government, and vacation travelers

- Max. LTV – 65% to 70%.

- Max. amortization – 20 to 25 years.

- Min. DSCR – 1.40x.

- Min. occupancy – 60% over the past three years.

- Max. Occupancy when calculating room revenue – 75%.

- Min. furniture, fixtures and equipment (FF&E)
– the greater of actual of 5% of total revenue.

- Min. franchise fee – the greater of actual or 5% of total revenue.

- Min. maintenance fee – the greater of actual or 4.5% of total revenue.

- Capitalization rate – use market-driven
capitalization rate, typically 10% to 13%.

- Food and beverage (F&B) contribution should be less than 40%.

Limited Service Hotels

Includes limited service—midscale, limited service—economy, limited service—extended stay (e.g., Courtyard and Hampton Inn, Budget Inn, etc.). Caters primarily to business and vacation travelers, typically offers limited food services

- Max. LTV – 65% to 70%.

- Max. amortization – 20 to 25 years.

- Min. DSCR – 1.45x.

- Min.occupancy – 60% over the past three years.

- Max. occupancy when calculating room revenue – 75%.

- Min. furniture, fixtures and equipment (FF&E)
– the greater of actual or 5% of total revenue.

- Min. franchise fee – the greater of actual or 5% of total revenue.

- Min. maintenance fee – the greater of actual or 4.5% of total revenue.

- Capitalization rate – use market-driven
capitalization rate, typically 10% to 13%.

Suite/Extended Stay

Includes limited service, extended stay (e.g., Marriott Suites, Embassy Suites and Residence Inn, etc.). Rooms accommodate a longer stay than typical full or limited service hotels; rooms often have separate living, sleeping, and kitchen areas.

- Max. LTV – 65%.

- Max. amortization – 20 to 25 years.

- Min. DSCR – 1.45x.

- Min. occupancy – 60% over the past three years.

- Max. occupancy when calculating room revenue – 75%.

- Min. furniture, fixtures and equipment (FF&E)
– the greater of actual or 5% of total revenue.

- Min. franchise fee – the greater of actual or 5% of total revenue.

- Min. maintenance fee – the greater of actual or 4.5% of total revenue.

- Capitalization rate – use market-driven capitalization rate, typically 10% to 13%.

- Food & beverage (F&B) contribution should be less than 40%.

General Guidelines

Market and Location

The property should be easily accessible and visible from the highway or major roadway. Business-oriented hotels should provide ready access to downtown business areas, corporate parks, and airports. Vacation-oriented hotels should be highly visible from major roadways and be in close proximity to recreational amenities.

Property Condition and Characteristics

A stable historical operation of over 4 years is critical; properties less than 4 years old need to be carefully analyzed. The property should exhibit sufficient parking capacity to adequately accommodate its range of services and location.

The property should have an established, ongoing refurbishment program for both hard and soft goods.

Franchise affiliated hotels are preferable with franchise agreements extending beyond the term of the proposed loan.

Minimum acceptable occupancy (annualized for properties with seasonal fluctuations) is typically 60%; the average occupancy over the last 3 years should be at least 60%.

Normalizing Income and Expense Considerations

Income should be calculated based on the actual revenue collected during the most recent 12-month period (trailing 12) and should be stable in comparison to the previous 24-month historical average, including occupancy and average daily rate (ADR).

Adjustments to the income may include:

Recent strong hotel performance will in some cases result in the most recent 12-month revenue exceeding prior years significantly. Where this is the case, adjustments to stabilize the revenue over three years will typically be necessary.

Other Income may be included so long as the income is consistent with that generated by the property over the previous three years and is common for the market in which the property is located.

Adjustments to the expenses may include:

Increasing, decreasing, or normalizing the underwritten expenses based upon historical expense trends.

Consider applying an expense growth rate of 3% to represent escalation of expenses for the next 12 months.

Remove any insurance expense that is not specifically related to the real estate.

Remove any nonrecurring expenses from the underwritten expenses.

Reallocate any capital expenses from repairs and maintenance to capital expenditures.

Special Guidelines

Franchise/Type:

- Major, national flags.
- No regional/local brands, small chains, independents, B&Bs, resorts, etc.
- Typically ~45–100 rooms; typically interior corridor.
- Limited service (no restaurant or banquet rooms.)
- No MSA Tier 4 locations.

Loan Purpose:

- Refinance (preferred.)

- Acquisition. Property must demonstrate historic
cash flow to service the proposed debt.

- "Take-out" financing for start-up projects is strongly discouraged.

Feasibility ftudy required: 2–3 existing properties must provide
100% cash flow coverage of proposed debt. Additional properties
must guarantee proposed debt. Loan maximum is 60% of hard
costs. Loan cannot be securitized. Approval is unlikely.

Loan structure:

- Loan amounts of $1,000,000 – $6,000,000.

- Minimum equity injection of 15%.

- LTV maximum of 65%.

- Junior mortgages allowed by financial institutions only.

- Terms to 25 years IF property is <15 years old. Terms
to 20 years if property is >15 years old.

- "Cash out" situations allowed. Term.

Management:

- Majority of owners must have 5+ years of ownership AND
operator experience. Similar size and type of property (flag and
room count). Prefer experience in same (or very similar) market.

- Majority of owners must be "on site" and active in daily
management. No multicity/state operators; no investor deals.

- No significant break in service from the hospitality industry. No
"sabbaticals" in other industries before returning to motels.

Cash flow:

- Prefer minimum DSC of 1.15X. Excludes income
from billboards, cell towers, restaurants, etc.

- Minimum owners' salary of $30,000 per family.

Major Lender Guidelines

The following are the basic guidelines for hotel financing from a major lender that only works with banks and major financial institutions. If you decide to specialize in hotels, or if you get a hotel financing package from time to time, Coast Investors Capital, as a correspondent lender to this major institution, can structure and place the loan for you. You would be the broker of record and receive your full brokerage fees.

FRANCHISE: Hotel franchise must be nationally recognized, limited service, midscale franchise. Economy franchises are generally not acceptable, unless they are at the upper end of the economy segment. Full service properties will not be considered.

The following brands generally meet the targeted franchise profile. Those in bold type currently have the strongest market appeal.

Economy/Budget

Days Inn (Choice)
Econo Lodge (Cendant)
S leep Inn (Choice)
Super 8 (Cendant)
Travelodge (Cendant)
Baymont Inns (LaQuinta)
Microtel Inns (U.S. Franchise Systems)
Red Roof Inn (Accor)
Motel 6 (Accor)
Best Western (please contact us for separate Best Western credit guidelines)

Midscale (Limited Service)

Comfort Inn or Comfort Suites (Choice)
Fairfield Inn (Marriott)
Hampton Inn or Hampton Suites (Hilton)
Holiday Inn Express (Bass)
Howard Johnson (Cendant)
Hilton Gardens (Hilton)
Quality Inn (Choice)
Ramada Limited (Cendant)
Country Inn & Suites (Carlson)
Wingate Inn (Cendant)
AmeriHost (Cendant)
Staybridge Suites (Intercontinental)
Homewood Suites (Hilton)
Springhill Suites (Marriott)
AmeriSuites (Prime Hospitality)
Clarion (Choice)

LaQuinta (LaQuinta)_

DEAL SIZE:

Up to $6,000,000 (permanent loan amount). First mortgages will not exceed 65% of the eligible project cost.

LOAN PURPOSE:

Acquisition or refinance (preferred) of an existing stabilized hotel, including land, building, improvements, furniture and equipment, and project soft costs. Projects involving leased land will be considered on a case-by-case basis.

LOAN STRUCTURE:

Acquisition/refinance financing will be provided via a GECAF "direct" loan which represents first mortgage on the project. Junior mortgages, SBA 504, 7(a), or conventional financing are allowed by financial institutions only. Terms are subject to approval by GECAF.

GUARANTORS:

Personal guarantees may be required of all operating partners/shareholders regardless of ownership percentage. Corporate guarantees may also be required of any related affiliates. At a minimum, personal guaranties representing no less than 51% of the ownership are required. The requirement for personal/corporate guarantees is primarily based on the operating experience and strength of the guarantor rather than the ownership percentage.

TERM:

Up to 25 years fully amortizing on the GE Capital first mortgage.

PROPERTY PERFORMANCE:

The property to be acquired/refinanced must evidence satisfactory and/or stabilized financial performance as defined with historic debt service coverage of 1.15:1 or greater (excludes income from billboards, cell towers, restaurants, banquet rooms, etc.).

Turnarounds, nonperforming and unstabilized properties will not be considered. A minimum owner's draw of $30,000 is required.

MANAGEMENT/OWNERSHIP EXPERIENCE:

Existing hotel projects must include one or more principals with majority ownership that can demonstrate proven hotel ownership **AND/OR** management experience of either a similar national hotel franchise or a similar size non-franchise within the last 5 years. The prior experience ownership/experience must be verifiable. Owner/operator must reside in the subject market prior to closing and plan to be involved in the subject operations on a daily basis. Properties operated by third party management companies will not be considered.

INVESTOR DEALS:

Investor deals are generally prohibited, e.g. deals with principals who either have no prior hotel management/ownership experience but are investing capital into the project. Deals that involve one or more principals who derive the majority of their taxable income from owning/operating multiple hotels will be considered on a case-by-case basis.

CAPITAL INJECTION:

Existing hotel projects require a minimum of 15% capital injection towards the eligible total project cost.

AGE OF PROPERTY:

Property should be less than 15 years old. Interior corridor properties are preferred over exterior corridor properties. Older properties with major renovation can be eligible.

APPRAISAL/FEASIBILITY STUDY:

An appraisal/feasibility report may be required to be performed by an MAI certified appraiser on an existing hotel project if the project involves any "conversion" aspects. Borrower supplied appraisal/feasibility reports will not be acceptable. Property should have excellent location, visibility, accessibility, and positive economic demand generators. Generally, property demand must rely less than 40% on leisure travel.

CHAPTER FOURTEEN

Self-Storage Properties Underwriting Guidelines

Earlier in this book we defined "cap rate." It is the primary driver of value in real estate investments and is particularly pertinent to our discussion of self-storage properties.

The Role of Stabilized Income in the Cap Rate

The "stabilized income" when used in the calculation of value is the income after expenses and proper adjustments such as depreciation, amortization, and personal expenses. The resulting number is referred to as your net operating income (NOI). Cash flow is what you put in the bank after you pay the loan but before you pay federal and state taxes.

What does the word "stabilized" mean in relation to income? When considering value for a sale purchase or refinance, the income that produces the value must be stable. In other words, a loan underwriter is looking for steady income, preferably increasing income, without major up or down movements.

There are shortcuts people use in developing values for self-storage and other real estate. The most common is the "trailing 12 months" cap rate. This tactic simply substitutes the average of the previous 12 months' NOI for a stabilized one. The assumption is that nothing significant in the facility or market will change. This approach, though basic, gives the underwriter a picture of what should be, and then adjustments can be made.

Below are some ratios and adjustments used in the self-storage market. If you are going to select this sector of the market as your primary niche, you need to become well acquainted with the industry and its lenders. A good place to start is www.insideselfstorage.com.

Underwriting Profile

Includes mini-storage, climate controlled, other self storage

- Max. LTV – 70% to 75%.

- Max. amortization – 25 years.

- Min. DSCR – 1.30x to 1.35x.

- Min. vacancy reserve – the greater of actual or market vacancy, typically 7% to 15%.

- Min. replacement reserves – the greater of actual or $0.15 to $0.25 per square foot.

- Capitalization rate – use market-driven capitalization rate, typically 9% to 11%.

General Guidelines

Property Condition and Characteristics

The property should be designed and configured for ease of entry and egress by tenants, including access by 18-wheel tractor trailers.

Buildings of low-quality construction or with poor insulating capacity are discouraged.

Foundations and driveways should be reinforced concrete (4" - 3,000 psi) with fiber mesh reinforcing.

Property will be perceived as "safe." Entry to the property will be through an electronic gate with some type of key-pad entry and exit. The entire property will be lighted, especially interior hallways and outside storage, with all common area lighting controlled by timers. Individual units should have quality hasps and locks. Surveillance cameras, if provided, will be installed at the entrance and exit gates.

The property should have adequate traffic exposure and a desirable average daily traffic (e.g., 15,000 cars per day).

Minimum acceptable occupancy (annualized occupancy for properties with seasonal fluctuations) is typically 85%.

A stabilized occupancy and operating history is preferable.

Normalizing Income and Expense Considerations

Calculate potential gross income (PGI) by adding the annual in-place revenue generated by the current tenants plus the annual income generated from vacant space at market rent. Then apply the appropriate vacancy reserve to calculate effective gross income.

Income should be calculated based on the actual revenue collected during the most recent 12-month period.

Adjustments to the income may include:

Mark to market any rents from leases that are written above or below market rent (e.g., if a tenant pays $4.00/SF and the market rent for comparable properties is $3.00, consider adjusting the rental income to $3.00/SF).

Consider subtracting any rental income from any tenant who is 60 days or more delinquent.

Include expense reimbursements, CAM, and other income (e.g., yard storage, parking fees, and ancillary services.)

Adjustments to the expenses may include:

Expenses will be calculated based on the actual expenses during the most recent 12-month period.

Increase, decrease, or normalize the underwritten expenses based upon historical expense trends.

Apply the greater of the actual or market management fee whether the property is professionally managed or owner-managed, typically 2% to 4%.

Consider applying an expense growth rate of 3% to represent escalation of expenses for the next 12 months.

Remove any insurance expense that is not specifically related to the real estate.

Remove any nonrecurring expenses from the underwritten expenses and reallocate any capital expenses from repairs and maintenance to capital expenditures.

CHAPTER FIFTEEN

Healthcare Underwriting Guidelines

Underwriting Profile

Nursing Home, Congregate Care, Assisted Living, Other Healthcare

- Max. LTV – 70% to 75%.

- Max. amortization – 25 years.

- Min. DSCR – 1.30x to 1.35x.

- Min. vacancy reserve – the greater of actual or market vacancy, typically 5% to 10%.

- Min. replacement reserves - the greater of actual or $250 to $350 per bed.

- Min. uccupancy requirement – typically 85%.

- Capitalization rate – use market-driven capitalization rate, typically 9.5% to 11.5%.

General Guidelines

Market and Location

Adequate linkage factors to retail services (including food, drugstore and community shopping) within a 3-mile radius.

Adequate community services (such as fire, police, schools, and health facilities) within a 10-mile radius.

Scrutinize properties located in economically depressed, seasonal, or resort-oriented areas.

Property Condition and Characteristics

Properties with more than one story should have elevator service.

Properties should exhibit acceptable aesthetic qualities to be competitive with market standards; inferior physical characteristics are less desirable and may require a higher interest rate spread and higher underwriting constraints and reserves.

Property must comply with ADA requirements.

Property should provide a variety of services for residents such as meal service, transportation, religious services, and activity programs, along with a wide range of ambulatory and some nonambulatory services.

Normalizing Income and Expense Considerations

Calculate potential gross income (PGI) by adding the annual in-place revenue generated by the current tenants plus the annual income generated from vacant space at market rent. Then apply the appropriate vacancy reserve to calculate effective gross income.

Income is typically calculated based on the actual revenue collected during the most recent 12-month period or per a current rent roll certified by the borrower.

Adjustments to the income may include:

Mark to Market any rents from leases that are written above or below market rent (e.g., if a tenant pays $500/unit/month and the market rent for comparable properties is $350/unit/month, consider adjusting the rental income to $350/unit/month).

Subtract any rental income from any tenant who is 60 days or more delinquent.

Storage, parking, meals, transportation, laundry and other income should be consistent with the historical income generated by the property for the past two years.

Vacancy and Collection Loss

Calculate a vacancy and collection loss factor based on a review of the following:

- Apply the greater of the current market or economic vacancy; analyze actual collection losses at the property over the past two years.

- Analyze the creditworthiness of the existing tenant base, including percentage of Medicare and Medicaid subsidization.

- Analyze the number of short-term or month-to-month leases.

- Historical review – analyze all income and expense trends; explain any significant increase or decrease over 5% per annum.

- Analyze any other factors that may affect the collectability of future rents.

Adjustments to the expenses may include:

Increasing, decreasing, or normalizing the underwritten expenses based upon historical expense trends.

Apply the greater of the actual or market management fee whether the property is professionally managed or owner-managed; typically 3% to 5%.

Consider applying an expense growth rate of 3% to represent escalation of expenses for the next 12 months.

Remove any insurance expense that is not specifically related to the real estate.

Remove any nonrecurring expenses from the underwritten expenses.

Reallocate any capital expenses from repairs & maintenance to capital expenditures.

CHAPTER SIXTEEN

Mobile Home Park Properties Underwriting Guidelines

Underwriting Profile

MHP 1 Star, MHP 2 Star, MHP 3 Star, MHP 4 Star, MHP 5 Star

- Max. LTV - 80%.

- Max. amortization – 25 to 30 years.

- Min. DSCR - 1.20x to 1.25x.

- Min. vacancy reserve – the greater of actual or market vacancy; typically 5% to 10%.

- Min. replacement reserves – the greater of actual or $35 to $75 per pad.

- Min. occupancy requirement – typically 85%.

- Capitalization rate – use market-driven capitalization rate; typically 9% to 11%.

General Guidelines

Market and Location

Desirable neighborhood near shopping amenities.

Adequate linkage factors to retail services (including food, drugstore, and community shopping) within 3-mile radius.

Adequate community services (such as fire, police, schools, and health facilities) within a 10-mile radius.

Scrutinize properties located in economically depressed, seasonal or resort-oriented areas.

Property Condition and Characteristics

Should include off-street parking, and the units should be modern, late model coaches.

Park may include single- and double-wide skirted coaches in good condition with concrete patios or raised porches; the streets should be paved.

Parks that derive more than 25% of annual gross income from rent attributed to "park owned" units may be limited to a fully amortized loan with a term not exceeding the average remaining economic life of the park-owned units.

Amenities should be well-maintained and sufficient to compete with rental alternatives in the local housing market. Park should be attractively landscaped, and streets should be gravel or paved and in good repair.

Parks with no more than 10 pads per acre density are typically preferred.

Generally, minimum parking ratio of 2.0 spaces per pad, depending on classification of park, number of amenities, and common areas.

Property should have demonstrated a strong ability to resell existing homes over the past two years.

Coaches for sale will not account for more than 15% of total pads.

Rented homes owned by the park will not account for more than 15% to 20% of total pads.

Leases are typically short term in nature, often month-to-month.

Properties should exhibit acceptable aesthetic qualities to be competitive with market standards; inferior physical characteristics are less desirable and may require a higher interest rate spread and higher underwriting constraints and reserves.

Normalizing Income and Expense Considerations

Calculate potential gross income (PGI) by adding the annual in-place revenue generated by the current tenants plus the annual income generated from vacant space at market rent. Then apply the appropriate vacancy reserve to calculate effective gross income.

Income is typically calculated based on the actual revenue collected during the most recent 12-month period or per a current rent roll certified by the borrower.

Adjustments to the income may include:

Mark to market any rents from leases that are written above or below market rent (e.g., if a tenant pays $75/pad/month and the market rent for comparable properties is $55/pad/month, consider adjusting the rental income to $55/pad/month).

Consider subtracting any rental income from any tenant who is 60 days or more delinquent.

Storage, parking, laundry. other Income – the income should be consistent with the historical income generated by the property for the past two years.

Vacancy and Collection Loss

Calculate a vacancy and collection loss factor based on a review of the following:

- Apply the greater of the current market or economic vacancy.

- Analyze actual collection losses at the property over the past two years.

- Analyze the creditworthiness of the existing tenant base.

- Analyze the number of short-term or month-to-month leases.

- Historical review – Analyze all income and expense trends; explain any significant increase or decrease over 5% per annum.

- Analyze any other factors that may affect the collectability of future rents.

Adjustments to the expenses may include:

Increase, decrease, or normalize the underwritten expenses based upon historical expense trends.

Apply the greater of the actual or market management fee whether the property is professionally managed or owner-managed, typically 3% to 5%.

Consider applying an expense growth rate of 3% to represent escalation of expenses for the next 12 months.

Remove any insurance expense that is not specifically related to the real estate.

Remove any nonrecurring expenses from the underwritten expenses.

Reallocate any capital expenses from repairs and maintenance to capital expenditures.

Section II

MARKETING FOR MILLION$

CHAPTER SEVENTEEN

The Marketing Process

In the previous chapters we provided you a significant amount of information regarding the different kinds of properties and commercial mortgages available. Now comes the difficult part, the *marketing process!*

Once you have decided what area of commercial mortgage finance you want to specialize in, you must develop your marketing plan in order to get applicants for your loans.

To develop a marketing plan you must know who your target audience is and then go after them.

In this section, I provide you with an overview of marketing, plus the tools of the trade you can use to attract clients. You will accomplish far more with a targeted plan of action than with random attempts. Allow me to guide you through the steps and considerations you need to take to come up with a successful marketing plan.

Financing Value Proposition

A good value proposition is a clear statement that convinces a prospect to become a client. It will articulate the benefits and experiences the customer should expect to receive from you, with what tradeoff, at what cost, and how that value proposition is superior to other viable choices.

The way you present your value proposition must be prepared, rehearsed, re-rehearsed and delivered in an Academy Award–winning presentation that will make your prospect truly believe your financing proposal is the one for them. That's right. If you want to make sales easily, you need to develop your acting skills. If you don't believe me, just look around at the top performers in any company. You will see them put on an act worthy of an Oscar award when they pitch their products.

Creating Your Difference

What can you offer your prospect in your value proposition that is different than what the company down the street has to offer? If you have researched your investors and negotiated wholesale terms with them, then you should be able to offer competitive financing products to your borrowers. In the age of the Internet, you simply must offer competitive terms to get the client. The rest is service; service consists of politeness, respect for the needs of the client, and keeping in touch with the client as needed to follow through on your commitments.

Selling Your Differences by Understanding Profiles

Types of customer profiles

Profiles can be economic, demographic, or behaviorally based, and the difference is very important to your business. If you have a profile of your best customers then you should look for new customers that fit that profile. Let's assume you have decided to specialize in owner-occupied business financing. The best demographic profile for a potential client is as follows: 1) a person who owns his own business; 2) the business he owns requires an office (doctor, chiropractor, insurance agent) or a warehouse (contractor, importer, exporter, distributor, light industrial company); 3) the client already owns the real estate (prospective refinance client) or is actively looking to purchase. The problem is that there are over 34 million small businesses that fit that profile, so your job is to refine the search and find the ones that need your services.

Customer behavior is a much stronger predictor of your future relationship than demographic information ever will be. Therefore a business owner that is searching the Internet for property or for lenders is a better profile than a business owner who is just minding his business. Therefore your first marketing move must be the creation of a website.

Developing a Marketing Website

Once you've identified your market, your next step will be to develop a great website. Your website must be specifically designed to sell your product. Everything within your website should have one purpose—getting your visitor to take action. In other words, you want your website visitor to fill out a quick application for a commercial mortgage, or to at least sign up for a monthly newsletter about finance and the real estate market.

The quick application filled out by the visitor will be your lead to call this potential client and start building a client file. Your application should be as simple as possible, yet have sufficient information about the property being purchased or refinanced for you to make an educated guess about the viability of your potential client.

Here is the basic information you need to ask for on your quick application:

- Contact data
- Business type
- Years in business
- Profitability level
- Type of property (office, warehouse, retail etc.)
- Purchase price
- Down payment
- Requested loan
- When is loan required?
- Borrower Credit (over 700, 660-699, 630-659, 600-629, less than 600.)

The *CRES Solutions* CD contains a Quick Application form, already built for you, which is capable of servicing multiple product and client types.

Writing Effective Website Sales Copy

Words are the most powerful marketing tool you have. The right words will turn your visitors into customers. The wrong words will cause them to go away and never return.

Your words are the entire foundation of your business. Your product, your website, and your marketing strategies all depend upon your words. Fancy graphics don't make sales—the right words do.

Every word, sentence, and headline should have one specific purpose—to lead your potential customer to fill out that quick app form or pick up the phone and call you. Write your website copy as if you are talking to just one person. Identify a problem and validate that one visitor's need for a solution. Continue to explain why your financing is the solution to their problem. Tell them exactly what your financing will do for them—why it will solve their problems and how. Pack your copy with benefits and more benefits. Write to persuade—that's the bottom line.

Your words are the entire foundation of your business. Your product, your website, and your marketing strategies all depend upon your words. You must learn how to write persuasive words specifically written for your target customer. You must feel your customer's needs and write your copy with passion, excitement, and loads of benefits.

Text: Your text should be written in a black, legible font with a light background. Avoid using fancy fonts or backgrounds that will make your text difficult to read. When you begin writing, write in small blocks of text with a space between each block. There is nothing that will make your visitor click away faster than a sea of black text, so make sure you use plenty of white space.

Headlines: Begin your website sales letter with a powerful headline that demands attention. This headline is the most important part of your entire sales letter. If it doesn't grab your potential customer's attention, they won't bother to read the rest of your letter. Your headline should be displayed in a larger bold font and demand your potential customer's attention.

Subheadings: Use subheadings (headlines) throughout your website sales letter to capture the attention of those who just scan your text. Your subheadings should provide highlights of each section of your sales letter and be displayed in a larger, bold font.

Introduction: Once you've captured your potential customer's attention with your powerful headline, you should now direct their attention to your introduction. Write a brief paragraph about your financing to let them know exactly what you have to offer them. Keep your introduction brief and to the point with no filler content.

Body Copy: Once you've written your introduction, continue to tell your potential customer why your financing is the solution to their problem. Tell them exactly how your financing will benefit them. Identify a specific problem and promote your financing as the solution. This can be accomplished with a series of questions that identify a specific problem that your financing will solve. Ask your potential customer questions that you know they can identify with—feel their needs.

Every word, sentence and headline should have one specific purpose—to lead your potential customer to your order page. When writing your sales copy, direct your words to the individual. Use words like "you" and "your" rather than "them" or "their." Write as if you are speaking with them one-on-one. Again, the bottom line is write to persuade.

Here's a convenient formula to use when writing your website sales letter:

– Grab their attention—use a powerful headline that demands attention.

– Create interest—pique their interest and create curiosity.

– Provide detail—provide details about your financing and services.

– Call for action—tell them to "fill out the quick app for a financing quote."

Many potential commercial borrowers are apprehensive about filling out a quick app, so make sure that your phone number is prominently displayed on each page of your website. You must put their mind at ease by displaying your full name, company name, and contact information. In addition, you must eliminate their sense of risk by avoiding high pressure tactics. When they initiate a telephone call to you, you can put their mind at ease by building their confidence in you and your product. In addition, include some of your testimonials or a "deals closed section" within your sales letter web page. Don't create a separate page for your testimonials, or they will be ignored. Place your testimonials throughout your sales letter to ensure their visibility.

Studies have shown that long sales copy out-sells short sales copy. However, some visitors do prefer a short sales letter. To accommodate both types of preferences, simply provide both. For those visitors who prefer a short sales letter, provide them with multiple opportunities (links) throughout your sales letter where they can click right over to your point-of-sale page.

When writing a long sales letter, keep in mind that with each additional click you will lose a percentage of your potential customers. Have you ever read a sales letter page that forced you to click through several pages to continue reading the sales letter? Many readers find this very frustrating and just click away. Try to keep your sales letter all on one page for the best results. Your visitors would much rather scroll through a long sales letter than click through and load another page. Their time is very valuable—accommodate them.

Call for Action/Free Offers

Once you've written your sales letter and packed it with all of the benefits your financing has to offer, your next step will be to "call for action." Ask for the order by asking them to fill out your quick app form or have them call your office.

For potential customers who still aren't convinced, provide them with free bonuses just for filling out your quick app. A great freebie idea is a downloadable booklet (valued at $14.95) about what you should know before buying and financing real estate.

Don't have a booklet or anything to offer? *Cresguide.com* offers a download service for brokers that can be installed on your website, allowing your client to receive a free download of the booklet he has selected as soon as he fills out the quick app or signs up for your newsletter. Your client will get to choose between several downloadable consumer booklets. The downloads, although free to the client, will cost you, the broker, from $0.50 to $0.31 per download. This is a small price to pay to obtain a lead.

P.S. Your final step will be to close your sales letter with a post script. When your visitor scans your sales message, chances are they'll read your headline, subheadings and your post script message. Place your most important benefits within your P.S. message. It will get read.

Write your words so they seamlessly flow from your beginning headline through to your quick app page. Pack your copy with all of the benefits your financing has to offer and keep it simple. Simple, well-designed sites with great copy make the most sales.

Paying For Traffic

Getting interested potential clients to your website is the next hurdle. Pay-per-click search engines such as Google, Ibank, and many others provide an extremely effective means of obtaining highly targeted traffic to your website. The concept is simple: you bid on targeted keywords for as little as .001 cents per click and receive targeted traffic to your website.

The most popular and probably most effective pay-per-click search engine is Google. As the market leader, Google's minimum bid is now 5 cents per click. But if you have strategically designed your website to sell, then paying only a nickel per visitor is a worthwhile investment.

The key to using pay-per-click services effectively is to focus on one specific financing type, and then select highly targeted keywords. This will help you weed out all of the window shoppers and attract your specific target audience.

Viewing Search Terms

Most pay-per-click search engines will enable you to view exact search terms that have been used by the general public to perform searches. Use this to your advantage. You can find out exactly what search terms are being used for your target market and place your bids accordingly. Try to create a list of as many relevant keywords as possible. The more keywords you bid on, the more traffic you will receive.

When bidding on keywords, keep in mind that in order to be successful, you don't have to be listed at the top. Although receiving a listing in the top three positions of the first page on Google will produce major traffic for your website, you must have a large advertising budget to compete for these choice top three spots.

Before placing your bid, perform a search to find out how much your competitors are paying per click. Try to place your bid so that your listing will appear on the first page; this increases your chance of success. By selecting highly targeted, less popular keywords, you'll not only attract a more targeted audience, but you'll also obtain a higher-ranked listing for less money.

Your Ad Copy

Your headline and advertising copy are the most important part of your entire strategy. Your headline must grab your potential customer's attention and force them to read on. Your copy should tell them exactly what you have to offer and convince them to visit your site. Avoid mentioning free stuff within your ads; this attracts freebie hunters, not serious clients. By weeding out those potential visitors who only want to get something for free, you will attract a more targeted audience of potential buyers. There is no need to pay for visitors who have no interest in buying anything in the first place.

Your ad listing should lead your potential customer directly to your product—your financing—without delay. In other words, if your financing isn't on your main page, then don't direct your potential customers to your main page. Why make them search for your product? Direct them to the page that contains your product information.

Reviewing Your Reports

Once your ad campaign begins, make sure you take the time to review the reports provided by the pay-per-click services. These reports inform you how well each of your keywords is performing, and thus enable you to adjust your keywords or change your bids accordingly.

To further increase your traffic, don't just stop with one pay-per-click search engine—try several at time. The more streams of traffic flowing into your site, the better.

Do an Internet search for pay-per-click search engines. Study each one carefully. For my money, Google, Yahoo and MSN are the only worthwhile options when it comes to general search engines. However, you will also want to investigate mortgage-specific search engines and lead origination sites.

If you're serious about your business and you're ready to drive a stampede of targeted traffic to your website, then give the pay-per-click search engines a try. They're well worth the small investment.

CHAPTER EIGHTEEN

Post Card and E-mail Marketing

The best direct mail marketing campaign you can create is a letter campaign. A series of personalized letters sent over time can be your most effective selling tool. The obvious drawbacks are that they are a lot of work, and they are expensive to create and execute.

So how do you stay visible to your customer without all that work and expense? One effective answer is post cards. By mailing post cards to each prospect or customer every three to eight weeks, your customers and prospects will think of you when they need something, and they will pick up the phone and call you when they are ready to buy.

Why Post Cards Are Hard Working Marketing Tools

They're Cheap to Produce.

Since a post card is usually a single sheet of paper, it's always cheaper than stuffing a letter and a brochure into an envelope. Post cards eliminate the additional costs of folding and inserting. You just print a name and address on one side and they're on their way to your customers.

The Postage Is Cheaper, Too.

They're cheaper to mail first class: only ?¢ each. This is the cost before postal discounts, which can be substantial! Strangely enough, post cards can be cheaper to mail FIRST CLASS than bulk. Restrictions do apply. They must be bar-coded and carrier-route labeled. If you use a letter shop to sort and mail, this service is done routinely for you.

Provide Fast Delivery of Your Message.

Mailing post cards allows you to take advantage of first class delivery while enjoying the postage savings off the first-class letter rate.

Save on Postage Even When Mailing Just A Few Cards.

Does your mailing list contain only a few hundred special people? Even when just mailing a few handfuls, post cards under 4-1/4" x 6" have a lower postage rate than first-class letters, even without any discounts.

Mailing House Costs Can Be Completely Offset By Postage Savings.

Tired of doing it yourself? If you take your post cards to a mailing house, their entire cost of inkjet addressing, tying, bagging, and delivering to the post office may still cost you less than if you mailed them yourself. It's like getting their service for FREE. You save money because their payment is recovered from all of the postal discounts they get for you. It's a win/win/win: you have less work, save money, and you get better delivery.

Post Cards Have High Readership.

Almost everyone reads post cards, even the mail-haters who throw out bulk direct mail at least glance at the post cards. By the time your prospects have the card in their hands, it's too late; they are going to look at it. You have to catch their attention in just a few words.

They're Diverse.

Post cards can be looked at as a piece of one-to-one communication, so you can be as personable or as formal as you want.

Four-Color Post Cards Are Cheap To Have Printed.

There are some gang-run post card printers (no, not that kind of gang) who print post cards en masse on giant sheets of 24" x 26" post card paper stock. The cost can be as low as $150 for 5,000 cards on E-Bay.

They're Easy to Handle.

Doing the mailing yourself? No stuffing, no folding. Not much messing around—just print, address, and mail.

Postcards can be used as hand-outs at trade shows. This really works. Make your case in a few lines and give it to your prospect at trade shows.

They Help You Remove Undeliverable Names From Your Mailing List.

Need to make address corrections in a timely fashion without additional expense? Send post cards first class with the imprint "Address Service Requested" below the stamp. The post office will return cards with undeliverable addresses to you. Lots of catalog companies do this before mailing their catalog—it's much cheaper to get cards back for free than to pay for getting wrecked and unusable catalogs back after the rough handling by the postal service.

Additional Recommendations for Post Card Usage

There are three hard and fast recommendations for post cards. First, don't use cheap paper. Since post cards are usually small sheets, go for the good stuff. In short runs, paper stock is a small fraction of the overall costs. I rarely recommend cheap paper, except sometimes for longer press runs of 25,000 sheets and up, where paper cost is a much larger percentage of the overall campaign cost.

Second, don't go for gloss unless you are printing in four colors. A glossy finish will get marked, mangled, and scarred at the post office—gloss cards aren't handled well by the post office automatics. Use crisp, bright-white 80 pound linen stock.

Finally, size matters. Use a card which is at least 5-1/2" x 8-1/2". This size gets attention, and it is the largest size you can mail without incurring additional expense.

Creating Successful Cards Is Easy

Design your post cards for three levels of readership, as you would design any advertising sales copy.

The first level is a big bold headline to entice scanning readers. This copy is for folks who just glance at your card to get the idea. If you stop them with a clever headline, they'll continue reading. Your headline has one objective: to drive the reader into the rest of the copy.

The second level, subheads, are written and designed to intrigue and arouse the reader further. This line is not quite as large as the headline type and not quite as small as the body copy type. It encourages a smooth transition between the two areas. This line also has the same objective as the headline: to get them to read further.

The third level is your body copy. Keep the first line or two of the body copy smart and sharp—written and designed, of course, to keep the reader reading. The transition from scanning reader to confirmed reader has not yet taken place. The first few lines of body copy must be clever enough to accomplish this transition. Get the reader hooked in the first few lines and he will read the rest. Now you can start selling your objective. Don't forget to tell the reader exactly what you want him to do, and be specific. Do you want him or her to contact you via telephone for further information, or would you rather the reader write or fax you for more information?

Tips to Remember:

At the bottom of the post card your logo may be equal in size but not larger than your telephone number. The phone number should be in large enough type to be seen clearly if the card is lying on a desk.

If you print "Save This Card!" somewhere near the top, people will do it. It's amazing—if you don't print this line, they won't.

It's okay to send a card more than once. Successful cards can be sent forever as long as they continue to cover their costs. Unsuccessful cards or hard-to-track cards can still be sent regularly. You get sick of looking at them long before your customers get tired of receiving them. If any customers complain, at least you know you're getting noticed.

Bring in some visual recognition when creating a multicard campaign; keep the image and the message the same on the address side of each succeeding card.

It's usually institutional copy on this side anyhow, like name, address, phone, etc. The address side is also a good place for a few bold lines of ad copy or a free offer to the reader to get more information, such as, "Call now to get our free booklet about financing commercial real estate."

Don't forget, a post card campaign is not a single mailing; a campaign, by definition, is a sustained effort. So mail your cards out frequently. Above all, direct mail is a numbers game; mail as many cards to as many people as you possibly can.

E-mail Marketing

It has become increasingly harder to promote a business using e-mail. Spam clogs up in-boxes and most people are quick to delete the deluge of mail they receive without even reading it.

Nonetheless, e-mail marketing, if done correctly, can be an inexpensive and quick way of reaching a very large audience. The key is to get people to WANT to receive your mailings. To do this, you need to do permission mailing. Permission mailing means having people sign up on your web site to receive informational e-mails, or they can provide their e-mail addresses when they purchase something from your company. In this way, you can collect e-mail addresses without buying a list that may have been created and/or sold illegally.

E-mailing advertisements (with permission) can still become redundant, and the recipient will likely ask to be taken off the mailing list unless you:

- Offer relevant content to the real estate investor. Good ideas are interest rate trends, business trends, and news.

- Offer new tips and information on business needs and interest rate trends regularly.

- Provide very targeted mailings.

- Send news of new financing programs.

- Invite recipients to commercial financing seminars.

Two or three sentences of original content can provide potential customers a reason to read your e-mail. Original content also supports your advertising, which may otherwise be deleted. Establishing your own newsletter can draw the attention of your readers, and it only needs to be a few paragraphs long.

When e-mailing customers, you also need:

- A catchy headline

- A recognizable company name in the "from" box so they'll know it's from your business

- A simple one-click method for them to acquire more information on specific products or services

- A means of reaching your customer service.

Make use of the preview window provided by many e-mail providers. This is literally your "window of opportunity" to grab their attention. You may only have one second to capture the reader before he or she hits delete, so make sure something interesting shows up in that preview window. Make this about them. Unlike a press release, which tells the media what your business is up to, e-mail marketing needs to focus on benefits to the customer. Once you've got them reading, you can talk as much as you like about your company, further down the page.

A few e-mail marketing rules of thumb:

- Make sure everyone on the list has agreed to be there—don't add names without permission.

- Reassure readers that their information will not generally be shared.

- Give readers an opportunity to opt off of the list.

- Keep information concise, to the point, and focused on their needs.

- Don't blitz—emailing more than once a week can be annoying.

- Provide a choice of HTML or TEXT version.

Landing pages are also important. A landing page is where the reader goes to when he or she clicks on a link. Readers should be able to get more information by clicking on various links within the initial marketing e-mail or newsletter.

Make sure each link is specific to what the text is addressing at the point where the link is inserted into your e-mail. Don't send them to a home page and make them search for the specific information that brought them there; send them to the right landing page the first time. Amazon.com is an excellent example with targeted landing pages. If you click on a specific book you will get a page with details and reviews of that book as well as suggestions for similar books. That landing page provides price and purchase information and then leads to a sales page or shopping cart. Your promotional e-mails should do the same thing. Make sure you give your reader an opportunity to go to your home page as well by including it prominently in the letter.

Businesses work hard to build a customer base; retaining your valued customers should be one of your top priorities. One of the best ways to keep them coming back is to reach out to them regularly through an e-mail newsletter, to let them know just how valuable they are. It is one of the keys to any customer-retention strategy.

Sending a monthly or quarterly e-mail newsletter is probably the easiest way to stay in touch with your customers. It is a great way to keep your clients abreast of the latest developments in your business, including sales, new product offerings, and seasonal deals. Include newsletter-only specials or coupons to generate interest in the newsletter, increase your subscriber list, and drum up sales.

Because so many of us are already overwhelmed by a daily deluge of e-mail, your newsletter needs to be offer more than just ads for your products. Include informative articles, interviews, or other information to entice your subscribers and make it a worthwhile read.

Put yourself in your customers' shoes and try to determine what kinds of information would prove valuable to them. If your company sells collectibles, for instance, a survey of market trends would be a great way to get your subscribers looking forward to each new issue.

If you are not a writer...

Or if you just don't have the time to generate the content yourself, you have options:

- You can seek permission to reprint existing articles,

- Or hire someone to write the content for you. *www.cresguide. com* offers mortgage professionals a private label newsletter service targeting the commercial real estate investor. To find out more about this service go to *www.cresguide.com/newsletterservice.*

Even if you can't commit to publishing a newsletter on a regular basis, you should still send out sporadic e-mails to inform your customers about your business and to remind them you're still there to meet their needs. This adds a personal touch to your business and lets your customers know you appreciate them.

To maintain good customer relationships, stay on the right side of spam law. This means offering your customers the ability to opt out of your electronic mailing or newsletter.

Implementing a double opt-in policy will ensure that your mailings are both welcome and legal. As the name suggests, a double opt-in policy requires users to say "yes" twice to their subscription request: once when they sign up (or make a purchase, if sign-up is integrated into your order process), and again to confirm the subscription. The confirmation usually comes in the form of an e-mail that requires a reply to complete registration.

The most valuable customer is the one you already have. In order to retain these customers, stay in touch with them and offer them incentives for continuing to patronize your company.

CHAPTER NINETEEN

Marketing with a Tele-Selling Campaign

Prospecting & Lead Generation

In addition to prospecting for leads through the Internet, you should also generate leads the old fashioned way—by reaching out and contacting them directly. Contact them via internet website, e-mail, telephone, mail, postcards, advertising or any other means you choose to incorporate into your overall marketing plan.

Your goal is always to convince the prospect to give you an opportunity to present your financing value proposition.

Remember, one of the big secrets of selling is to be in front of a qualified buyer when they are ready to buy, not when you need to make a sale. Therefore, find ways to keep your proposition in front of them often, so when they are ready, you will be in the right place at the right time.

You must be 100% sure you are in front of qualified prospects at the right time, with the right message, in the right format. Customers and prospects buy when they are ready to buy, not when salespeople need to make a sale—and especially not when pesky salespeople try to wear them down.

Think of your past successful sales. I'll bet that no matter what you sell, each customer you closed shared the following essential characteristics:

A need for your financing or service

An awareness of the need for it

A sense of urgency about obtaining it

Invest your time with the right people. The secret is to develop tools that will allow your prospect to respond to you when they are ready, interested, and motivated to do so.

We call this permission based prospecting. A far cry from bothersome phone calls, staged drop-in visits, and thinly veiled and contrived networking events, this process is proactive and positive.

How do you do this?

Start with a good contact management software system. There are several programs available for purchase. My own system is available on the *CRES Solutions* CD. Next, develop a strategy of frequent, yet unobtrusive ways to stay in touch with your key prospects. Worry more about making each contact count than about making a high volume of bothersome phone calls.

Don't pursue them to the ends of the earth to (a) create a need, (b) make them aware of the need, or (c) create a sense of urgency to make them buy.

If after three attempts to secure an appointment or a meaningful telephone conversation with a prospect you are still getting the brush-off, offer the prospect a free subscription to your information-packed valuable newsletter. By signing him up to your newsletter and providing him with valuable information he can use, you position yourself as an expert in the field. This increases your chances of getting the call when the prospect needs financing.

Newsletters, postcards, reports, information of value, audio tapes, CDs and other items that help prospects do what they do even better are some great ways to stay in front of potential customers in positive, productive, and powerful ways. The real secret is to give prospects a chance to respond to your varied offers. Be sure to include a fax-back form, 800-phone number, and response card with prepaid postage or even a return e-mail address that will allow your prospects to easily respond when they see how you can help them meet their needs. This prequalification is basically your close—done in advance! Your job is then to reach a mutual agreement that meets the customer's objectives, or to help them work through challenges they may face on a daily basis.

This strategy will yield a more positive perception, enhanced receptivity and a greater sense of professional acceptance. It is also far more sophisticated, less heavy-handed and more likely to succeed than the traditional notion that pitbull persistence pays off.

Remember:

- Prospects buy when they are ready to buy, not when you need to make a sale. So invest your time with the right people.

- Give prospects a chance to respond to your varied offers.

- Prequalification is basically your close—done in advance.

- Get in front of qualified prospects as often as possible.

Telemarketing and Cold Calling

It's obvious you can't physically see someone who is on the other end of a phone conversation. It is impossible to go through a physical financing presentation. Plus it's extremely difficult to size up a prospect's physical surroundings without being there. These ARE limitations. There is no denying that. But here are a few things to help you in spite of these phone-selling limitations:

The real, essential key to telephone conversation lies in one simple secret. Here it is: tone. The tone of someone's voice is a real tell-all secret as to how well you're doing. But it all starts with your tone. You need to be especially attentive to the tone that you use and then be finely tuned to the tonal response of your prospect.

Listen for background noise on the other end of the line. This simple, little secret can provide you real insight into how much attention your prospect is really paying to you and your message. Do you hear other conversations? How about the telltale sound of a computer starting up or shutting down? Always ask for permission to conduct a relatively lengthy phone conversation. Saying, "Do you have a few minutes so we might talk?" can go a long way towards guaranteeing a more responsive listener on the other end.

Never forget that all sales presentations are a two-way street. It is extremely easy to dominate the conversation on the phone because you have no way to judge the nonverbal response of prospects. However, engaging them and allowing them to respond allows you to judge their energy level and interest in the call. By conversing and playing an active role in the sales process, you will be generate more excitement and involvement from the client, and you will be better able to gauge their interest in the opportunity you are offering.

All of this leads us back to tone. Tone simply means the pace, intensity, pleasure or dissatisfaction, or the level of engagement displayed by your prospect. But remember—again—it all starts with your personal tone, not theirs. Pay attention to things like your use of pauses, speed of delivery, rate of response, articulation, and your receptivity to the person on the other end of the line. People will respond to you in the same manner and in the same tone that you give them.

What about phone scripts?

The real problem is that most of us aren't skilled script readers. The result is usually a stilted, one-way, constricted conversation that communicates no warmth, sense of engagement, involvement, caring, interest, or mutual trust. So,what is my advice to you? Forget the scripts!

If you master an understanding of the principles related to why someone would buy your financing or service, you will never need a script. Become an effective two-way communicator by knowing the benefits of your products and by listening to the concerns of your customer. Don't give them a prerecorded, canned, insensitive, one-way presentation!

23 Successful Techniques and Strategies

Here are 23 of the most successful techniques and strategies you can use to turbo charge your tele-selling campaign:

1. *Set goals*—establish guidelines for your telemarketing campaign. Be precise; set the number of calls and amount of time. Stay true to yourself by stopping at the end of your set time limit for the day.

2. *Block your time*—Make or return phone calls at precisely the exact time you committed to. Don't even be 2-3 minutes late! Have a game plan when you sell on the phone, and stick to it.

3. ***Make an agenda***—Preplan the phone call and make notes of the specific items you want to cover.

4. ***Telephone during "up" time***—Best times are 9 a.m. to 12 noon, 2 p.m. to 4 p.m. and never on Monday mornings or Friday afternoons.

5. ***Maximize the value of every call***—Before you speak to a prospect, have a predetermined game plan for all possibilities. If plan "A" doesn't work, you should be able to roll to plan "B" and "C" if necessary.

6. ***Know what you want to say***—Write a script only as a guideline; don't waste your time trying to memorize a "script." Instead, place your accent on increasing your prospect's business by providing answers and solutions to their biggest headaches.

7. ***Confirm your phone appointments***—Call ahead or send a note reminding the prospect of your upcoming phone appointment, and remind him or her of the agenda items to be discussed.

8. ***Sound and feel confident***—You've got something valuable to offer. Be articulate, pleasant, and confident. After all, everyone is looking for ways to increase their business.

9. ***Call the prospect by name***—Speak conversationally, identify the prospect's headaches and match them with solutions you have to offer. Stress the benefits of your financing or service. And never put down your competitors.

10. ***Take notes***—This allows you to keep a permanent record of the items discussed during the phone conversation.

11. ***Listen!***—This week is not good? Is next week better? Breakfast, not lunch? Scheduling problems? If not now, when?

12. ***Stay focused on the desired outcome***—Whatever the goal of this tele-selling campaign, try to close or confirm within 3 minutes. You must respect and value the prospect's time, so even when you get a face to face meeting, try to keep your presentations under 1 hour.

---

13. ***Don't try to close an "appointment" on the phone***—Stick to your game plan. Invite the prospect to a meeting; set an appointment for a presentation or demonstration. Don't get too ahead of yourself. Remember that selling is a process and not an event.

14. ***Be persistent without being obnoxious***—Listen to your prospect, learn to discern when you may be overstaying your welcome and quickly wrap up your call without appearing too pushy or overly aggressive.

15. ***Create a compelling message that gets return calls***—It's important to remember that you are trying to help a business improve its market share. People can tell the difference between someone who is trying to sell them something and someone who is genuinely interested in helping them succeed. When you leave voice messages, this should come across loud and clear.

16. ***Get to know the gatekeepers***—Develop positive, productive relationships with the people who screen your prospects' phone calls. Look for inside champions within your prospects' firms.

17. ***Respond, don't react, when dealing with a tough customer***—Use empathy. Disengage quickly, firmly, politely. Learn to use common objections as buying signals.

18. ***Learn to handle rejection***—Rejection is not personal. It is just a part of sales. Your financing is not for everyone. The ability to roll with the punches is the mark of a true professional.

19. ***Follow-up***—Have a follow-up strategy for each phone call you make. Use contact management software to help you keep track.

20. ***Conclude by recapping the main points***—Confirm any agreements reached during the conversation.

21. ***End each call on a positive note***—People are most likely to remember the last thing you say.

22. ***Send thank-you notes***—Express your gratitude for the time taken and interest shown by the prospect.

23. ***Make telephone selling a daily habit***—you will begin to enjoy it, and you will find yourself with more appointments than you ever imagined.

Whether you're calling to gain appointments or actually make the sale, these tips will help you get better results. Selling requires strong face-to-face skills, such as giving large group presentations, engaging in small group discussions, and commanding excellent one-on-one people skills. But selling also requires the ability to sell over the phone to people you can't even see!

Planning ahead is important. What key points do you want to make? Perhaps you wish to communicate how your financing solves a specific customer problem, how easy it is to use, or the cost savings your financing can yield. Most experts suggest limiting the number of key points in any presentation to three. Whether you are meeting face-to-face or over telephone, determine your key points, and be prepared with your supporting material. This is especially important on telephone calls, because your time is more limited than in face-to-face interactions. You don't want to waste valuable phone time hunting around for the documents which common sense should have told you that you would need for that call. Have them ready!

CHAPTER TWENTY

Seminars and Other Creative Marketing Techniques

As part of your marketing strategy, strongly consider offering both mini-seminars and day-long seminars. A miniseminar is when we are invited to speak about our products, services, or the real estate market as a whole. Full seminars instruct real estate investors how to find, buy, and finance profitable investment real estate. If you do not know how to host a seminar, CRES Seminars can either do the whole thing for you or sell you a comprehensive kit with all the tools you need to conduct a successful commercial real estate investor seminar, including how to rent the right facilities, invite the proper audience, and present valuable content that will be remarked on afterwards by influential real estate professionals. Seminars to real estate investors and commercial real estate brokers are a very successful way of getting your name in front of many influential real estate people. Any one of them may be your customer in the future or may pass your name to a friend or associate.

Thousands of residential mortgage brokers and financial consultants have attended seminars structured using the CRES system. CRES Seminars can implement a strategy to make your financing packages the best known products in your marketplace. Seminars are a great way to market your product.

CRES seminar marketing system is the result of years of developmental research on prospecting, direct mail response rates, e-mail campaigns, and internet marketing. Every detail has been examined, designed, field tested, and fine-tuned to provide the highest possible response rates.

A desirable seminar is one with limited seating availability. Accordingly, when you send someone an invitation, make sure that it says that seating is limited and that they need to call to RSVP.

Envelopes That Get Opened

Wedding style looks get opened—no one dares to miss the party! Your address (without name) imprinted in fancy script on the back flap of envelope. Real stamps! No bulk rate decals or postal metering that scream JUNK MAIL! The recipient's name and address should be imprinted on front in blue fancy script that looks handwritten. The required bar code is printed in black and moved to lower corner to prevent this mailing requirement from marring the look.

Mailing Lists of Real Investors

If you purchase a mailing list, do so from a good source. Direct mail professionals will tell you that the dollars are in the data! Shop around and ask questions as to how the lists were accumulated, how old they are, what is their target market? Ask specific questions that suit your target market.

The Chocolate Jar Marketing

In my early days, I owned a small securities brokerage firm that sold corporate bonds to institutional investors. My clientele was comprised of insurance companies, pension funds, banks, and other major players. That market is controlled by the "big boys" of Wall Street because institutional buyers do not want to deal with small firms with limited liquidity. When an investor gave me an order he became my client, and, as a client, he was placed on my mailing list. Each month I would send each of my clients a small glass jar with my company name and logo outside. Inside, the jar it was full of Hershey's Chocolate Kisses. When the jar was empty, my clients would often use it to hold pens, pencils, or they would refill the jar with goodies. I also sent a jar of chocolate to all potential clients whose business I was seeking, but who had not yet given me an order.

One of my potential clients was a large bank in Dallas, located less than a mile from my office. For months I tried to talk to the head honcho at the trading desk, but to no avail. I started sending him a chocolate jar after every call I made to his office. Several months passed with no result, until one day, my secretary came running into my office, all excited because the head honcho was on line two. I excused myself from the call I was on, and spoke with Mr. Honcho. He immediately said, "Listen, this is the big honcho at so-and-so bank. You have been sending me a jar full of chocolate for months and I have never taken your call. I like a guy with perseverance, so be here for lunch tomorrow and I will introduce you to my top traders." I was so thrilled to finally make that contact that I did not sleep at all that night. The following day I went to the bank to meet with Mr. Honcho, and when I walked into the trading room I saw my empty jars on many of traders' desks. From that day on, Mr. Honcho and his traders became one of my best clients. This confirmed to me that perseverance with respect will get you in the door eventually. Financing knowledge, service and competitive pricing will keep you in.

The Art of Commercial Mortgage Brokering

CHAPTER TWENTY ONE

Asking for the Sale

Small Business Sales—Dealing with the President

Selling is more a function of asking than of telling, of questioning rather than presenting. People buy for their reasons rather than for a salesperson's reasons. You should ask several questions throughout your sales call and presentation that will help you understand the prospect's buying motivations. These motivations are important because if you focus on the motivations as well as the agenda of your prospect, you will stand a much better chance of finalizing a transaction. Starting with broad questions, then moving towards more narrow ones is another principle that is extremely useful. Broad questions tend to be less threatening than narrow questions. Easy-to-answer questions will encourage your prospect to open up to you. People tend to avoid anything they do not understand, and your prospect is no different, so start with these more general questions in order to produce more general information.

After you have gained a basic understanding of your prospect's needs, you should move on to more detailed questions that will allow you to point ways that your financing or service can aid the prospect. Use easy-to-comprehend questions—don't use fancy vocabulary that the customer may not be familiar with; this could damage your chances of a sale. (Wow, look at me I know all these fancy words!)

Asking the right questions will help you to guide the interview and presentation and keep the tone positive. Some prospects might tend to continually stray away from the subject at hand—your sale—but if you know what you're doing when asking questions, you can avoid this time-consuming practice.

You can keep the tone of your interview positive by asking questions in a way that allows your prospect to agree with you. Studies have shown that most people prefer to agree than to assert themselves to disagree.

The single, most dynamic and powerful question to ask your prospect is this:

"What is the most critical issue affecting your financing needs?

This question really cuts to the core of the issue. It allows your prospect (and you) to get to the heart of their problem, need, agenda, or irritation. This question allows you to build to follow-up with additional questions, based strictly on their response. These questions might include: "Why do you say that?" or "What else causes you concern?" or "If that were solved, how would it make your life/job easier?"

Finally, but most importantly, you should ask your questions, but be quiet and listen as the prospect attempts to answer them. Interruptions will, without a doubt, turn your prospect off. This may seem obvious to most, but you cannot listen to the prospect's needs while you are talking. Therefore, let your prospect do most of the talking as you are interviewing him or her. This will surely increase your chances of finalizing the transaction.

To summarize these key points: Ask questions to find buying motivations. Start out with broad questions and then narrow down. After asking questions, be quiet and listen to the prospect's response.

Nothing Happens Until You Ask for the Sale

A successful salesman has to overcome several common sales maladies before asking for the sale. The three maladies of a salesman are: tension, resistance, and objections. Each has its own unique role to play and needs to be identified and dealt with in the context of a sale.

1. *Tension*—the level of dynamic, kinetic aggression that exists between the salesperson and prospect in any sales interaction.

2. *Resistance*—the degree of negativity that either buyer or seller feels as related to the interaction and ultimate buying decision.

3. *Objections*—the tools used by the prospect to register the degree to which

the tension and resistance have been effectively reduced, to allow a clear path to a buying decision. There is a unique and causal relationship among these three very essential elements that occur in any sale.

As a sales professional, you need to know precisely when and how to ask the prospect to buy. By gauging the level of tension, resistance, and objection, you can determine the right moment to ask for the close. However, you must make sure you overcome all three maladies before you ask for the sale. *Tension*, *resistance*, and *objections* are elements of any sale. Use the following tips to help you tame them before you ask for the sale.

Overcoming the Maladies

Build trust—that way you are better able to sell value. If you seek only to be liked, you are only going to be able to sell price, not value. You must build value in the prospect's mind, and this begins with building trust. Never quote price before you have created a perception of value. If value exceeds price, you will make a sale. If it does not, you won't. It's that simple.

Don't confuse the buyer—if you offer them too many choices, they will make no choice at all. Limit options and make strong, accurate recommendations. This is far more effective than offering a broad range of choices.

Use Silence—after you make your presentation and handle any objections, go straight for the close by asking for the order. Ask a closing question such as, "Do you want the red one or the blue one?" Then shut your mouth.

Ask For the Sale

Finalizing the transaction occurs as a natural consequence of what has developed during the entire sales process; it is not something that happens merely at the end of the presentation. But you must ask for the purchase order at the end of the presentation. Without that question, there is no sale.

"Are you ready to get started filling out our loan application?"

If you find yourself hesitating to ask such a question, I'll suggest that your hesitance is a result of one of the following three factors: Either you have failed to determine the level of tension, resistance or objection involved; or you have failed to ask the correct qualifying questions; or you have failed to recognize the proper moment to ask for the sale.

Ask the prospect to buy when you are sure they won't turn you down! I recommend a conversational close versus a scripted close. However, there are a variety of closing techniques to choose from, ranging from hard sell to soft sell and everything inbetween.

Some of these include:

*A **direct close:*** Simply ask for the order when you are sure your prospect is ready. We can install the software as early as next week, would that be fast enough for you?

*A **deal/concession close:*** Using this closing technique gives the prospect the feeling they are making a smart choice and saving money (or getting more value). Use it with phrases like, "Order today and I can add this other module for only 10% more."

*A **time-driven close:*** This one works well with statements like, "Prices are going up next week, so you should go ahead a let me place your order today."

Trial offer: You can let the prospect use the financing at no risk for a trial period. This works well if you're selling products that make people's lives easier. They aren't likely to want to give it back if it has saved them a lot of time and effort during the trial period. On the other hand, if they haven't had the experience with the financing you told them they would have, then you probably won't get another chance. You need to master an understanding of these sales success principles, rather than attempt to memorize a series of tricks, maneuvers, scripted phrases, or canned responses. The truth is that once you master an understanding of the mindset and strategic principles involved with sales, you will be far ahead of the game.

Success in selling commercial mortgages is more a function of understanding its science and strategy than of mastering secrets, scripts, or manipulative closing techniques. The fact is that the close happens well before the end of your presentation or pitch.

Chapter Twenty Two

Increase Your Name Recognition with Publicity and Advertising

Publicity is by far one of the most effective marketing tools at your disposal, but how do you promote yourself to the media so they will give your growing business the spotlight it needs?

Through storytelling. That's right, because ultimately, business stories are human interest stories and every reporter is looking for a good story. In fact, the press refers to the articles they write as stories. Here are 4 things you need to give the press to help them tell your story:

1. **Personality**. Create a personality for your company. The personality can be you or a character you create. Look at the mundane world of disability insurance. A talking duck gave that company personality. Sales grew over 30% per year. In any good story, the personality of the characters comes through. The press needs to get a sense of who you are in order to communicate that to the general public.

2. **Facts & Figures**. Reporters love facts and figures; they anchor a story in reality. However, if you prefer not to divulge sales figures, talk instead about your rate of growth. Say, "Our sales have doubled in the last year," or "We've already met our sales objectives for this year, and it's only July." Or better yet, "We are growing so fast I need to wear roller skates to the office just to keep up."

3. **Anecdotes**. As impressive as numbers can be, they are not the whole story. A real-life example of how you solved a client's problem brings your story to life. Readers want to hear about real people who manage to transcend their professional or personal problems, and readers want to hear about the people who helped them overcome the problem. Your story says I've been there. Tell the stories behind the facts and embellish them with details that would make someone want to listen (this is where drama comes in handy).

4. ***Details that Reveal.*** Reporters have their antennae up for interesting details about the people behind the companies. More and more, that's the approach reporters are taking, so you need to be open to sharing details. Maybe the contents of your refrigerator reveals something insightful about your marketing strategy, or you might reveal the fact that you work best in the nude. The motivation, and vision for your business is affected by your personality, hopes, quirks, and dreams. Consider which attitudes have served you best in creating business successes, and don't be afraid to discuss these personal details with the press.

Don't let isolation get to you; get out of the office and meet and mingle. I believe that isolation is the core obstacle to self-promotion. We stop making contact, avoid people we don't feel like talking to, and then wonder why the phone isn't ringing. To turn that trend on its ear, go out of your way to get into conversations with anyone and everyone you can—in person, on the phone or via e-mail. Cross the street, cross the room, or cross the train to talk to someone.

All it takes to start a conversation is a question, any question. One day last week all it took was a sneeze for me to begin a conversation with a potential prospect. Once you've opened up a conversation, find out what that person is working on, and tell them what you're working on.

If you are more comfortable writing an e-mail than talking in person, initiate dialogues by thanking people when you don't have to, or by acknowledging receipt of a message that doesn't necessarily ask for a response.

And follow up absolutely every single lead that comes your way, every person whose card you get, everyone who expresses even the slightest interest in your work. Don't worry about response. Just keep planting seeds and initiating conversations. Because anything, absolutely anything, can come out of a simple conversation: ideas, alliances, connections, referrals, new clients, new opportunities.

Press announcements: Whenever you close a new transaction do a press release to the local newspapers and the related trade magazine (of the industry your client is in.) If you introduce a new commercial mortgage program with low interest rates, or some other new feature, announce it! Create a section on your web site for your press announcements. These announcements give you the opportunity to look like a pro. Local newspapers will often run announcements of interest to the community they serve.

Referrals: As you network with other professionals, look for opportunities to exchange referrals. Set a goal to get acquainted with a new professional every week. That's 50 new opportunities for referrals a year. Improve your odds by going out and meeting new people. You never know when or where that great lead or suggestion or referral will come from, but knowing hundreds of people will vastly improve your odds. Make sure you find creative ways to stay in contact with these people. If you manage to stay fresh in their minds, they'll remember you when they learn of someone who might benefit from your services.

Speaking Engagements: You're an expert on certain topics of commercial real estate finance. The people you will speak to won't be. Meet the right people and organizations and offer to speak to their members at no charge. A 30-minute talk about financing for contractor yards at the local contractors association meeting could result in your providing real estate financing to several of the members. Look for opportunities to speak. Build your repertoire of talks. Hand out information sheets with your logo, your contact information, and your face printed on them. Offer your services to every club, association, and organization in your market. Doing so will improve your speaking abilities, improve the war stories you tell (as you add the humor, insight, and wit your audience injects into each new presentation,) and ultimately will build your reputation. Who knows? You might even be able to charge for your talks one day. But for now, use them to open doors and let listeners know that you're there to help them. And don't forget your business cards, flyers, and handouts (all of which contain your name and contact information).

Exhibiting at trade shows: If you are a broker offering commercial mortgages to owner occupied businesses, you should attend large conventions of the businesses that tend to own their own real estate. Restaurants, dry cleaners, chiropractors, insurance agents, distributors, contractors... Take your pick; there hundreds of likely categories.

Radio and TV: Television is the most powerful media available. Direct response TV (DRTV) refers to commercials made for TV in which viewers are asked to place an order during the advertisement through a toll-free number.

This contrasts with commercials where the objective is only to increase the visibility of the brand name.

There are two forms of DRTV: the short form, which is 1-2 minutes in duration, and the long form, which lasts 30 minutes. The long form is commonly referred to as an "infomercial."

TV is by far the most powerful medium available to advertisers. DRTV uses the unrivaled power of television to create the "impulse to buy." DRTV drives sales to retail, Internet, and other distribution channels.

DRTV has created overnight sensations and tremendous demand for products. Both the long and short forms of DRTV ads provide companies with immediate information about the effectiveness of their ads. This instantaneous feedback is available only through DRTV. If it's not working, you can change the ad immediately to get an improved response. And with a successful DRTV campaign you are building a loyal customer base of people who will continue to call you for their financing needs, allowing you to provide other forms of financing to small business.

CHAPTER TWENTY THREE

10 Steps to Ensure Your Success

1. Set Your Goals

Visualize what you want. A new car, a big house, $30,000 deposited in your bank account each month, a big boat, whatever. You can have whatever you want, but you must want it enough to work harder for yourself than you have ever worked for others. Set your goals, write them down, staple them in front of your work area, and set a target date for reaching them. Set short-term reachable goals and long-term higher goals. Be careful not to set them too high. This will cause you to become discouraged if you don't achieve them. Set your goals at achievable levels.

Work consistently towards accomplishing your goals each day, each week, and each month until you reach your short-term goals. Once you have attained your short-term goals, set them a little higher for the next time. Your short-term goals should all be aligned with your long-term goal(s). Thus, every short-term goal you achieve brings you a little closer to your long-term aims. Ultimately, you will achieve your long-term goals.

Goal setting is a must in every area of life.

2. Be Self-Disciplined

Get up early each day. Get ready for your job as if you were working outside your home. Each evening before you quit working, make a list of things you must do the following day. That way when you get up in the morning you are ready to go and ready to begin making money. This will give you an organized approach to each day. It's amazing how much you can get done using a "To Do" list. Many people get discouraged at the thought of creating an organized To Do list, but those same people spend a lot of time worrying about trying to remember what they need to do. Just write it down in an organized fashion—don't spend more time than you need to accomplish this—and you will find yourself less stressed because you will know exactly what you need to accomplish, and when.

3. Be Self-Motivated

Set up a schedule and stick to it. Be enthusiastic. Enthusiasm generates its own energy. Energy and good health are synonymous with motivated, happy people, or in other words, achievers.

4. Be Enthusiastic

Positive thinking will literally be your key to success. You have to convince yourself that you can succeed at whatever you desire. Because you can.

5. Do Not Allow Yourself to Become Discouraged

Remember, every "No" brings you closer to a "YES."

6. Schedule Your Time Wisely

A schedule is your roadmap to success. If you have no direction, you'll travel in circles and ultimately never reach your goals. Plan your work, then work your plan.

7. Have a Positive Attitude

Success is 90 percent attitude and only 10 percent aptitude. Learn the art of positive thinking because then you can do whatever you set your mind to. Do not allow negative thoughts to take over your mind. If you have a well-researched and designed business plan to earn yourself $x per month when fully executed, just stick to the plan and keep going.

8. Set up an Office Area

Most brokers work from their own homes, but it is still essential to set up a specified work area. Take pride in your business to ensure your success. As your business grows and you need assistants and other brokers to work for you, then you move to larger quarters.

9. Handle Your Money Wisely

Set up a written budget. Set aside a percentage of your business income to put back into your business. This is a must to grow your brokerage business.

Failure to reinvest your money will result in the failure of your business.

10. Take Care of Yourself

Get plenty of sleep, eat right, and exercise, even if it is only walking a mile a day. Remember to breathe deeply every time you feel frustrated, depressed, or feel you just want to quit and go back to that old dead-end job. Take some time to enjoy yourself with your family and friends. Be persistent. Persistence pays off. Don't give up.

Most businesses fail just at the moment they are about to succeed.

Brokering is the next to oldest profession in the world. And because it is one of the most basic forms of sales, it is one of the highest paid of all professions. If you don't believe me, look at Wall Street. Billion dollar fortunes have been built on brokering stocks.

The *Art of Commercial Mortgage Brokering* is a complete course on creating a successful brokerage business for yourself and your family. This course has taken you step by step through the entire process of selecting a brokerage niche, developing a marketing strategy, making the contacts of buyers and sellers, and building a valuable, long-lasting business. Everything you need to know to succeed is in these pages. These principles have worked for me in building my own business, and I encourage you to pursue your own dreams today.

This book is in your hands today because you have a desire to create a successful brokerage business. Use the tools I've provided you here, and on the companion CD, *CRES Solutions: Your Key to the Financial Vault*, to begin making your dream a reality. Remember, my companies, *www.cresguide.com* and *www.coastinvestors.com*, are here to provide you the support and services you need, particularly when you are just starting out in this industry. If you are willing to put in the time and effort, and if you adhere to the guidelines I have laid out for you in this book, then I know that you, too, can succeed as a commercial mortgage broker!

Section III

Appendices

Form & Letter Templates for Use in Commercial Mortgage Brokering

Appendix A: Your Broker Agreement

What follows is the most important document you will need to set up a successful brokerage business. This broker agreement ensures that you will get paid the commission you earn for your services. Simply fill it out with each borrower/client's information and have them sign it before you start working on their project.

Review the agreement carefully, so that you will know exactly what you have and have not promised your client. It is best to work with Coast Investors initially, to take advantage of their lender contacts and loan preparation services. Visit their website at *www.coastinvestors.com* for further guidance on using this agreement.

Broker/Coast Investors Exclusive Agent Agreement

This agreement is made June 25, 2005 by and between Coast Investors, LLC., hereinafter referred to as "Broker," and "ABC Real Estate Investors, LLC" hereinafter referred to as "Applicant," concerning the property described below hereinafter referred to as "Property."

Applicant and COAST INVESTORS hereby agree as follows:

Property Name: The Beach View Apartments

Property Address: 1234 Ocean Drive

Property Description: A 24 Unit apartment building consisting of 16 two bedrooms and 8 one bedrooms. Built in 1962 and remodeled in 1990.

Approx. Loan Request: $2,400,000

COAST INVESTORS AND BROKER AS APPLICANT'S AGENT

COAST INVESTORS is hereby engaged as Applicant's agent and are authorized to arrange financing for Property.

Applicant agrees that COAST INVESTORS is the exclusive agent to arrange financing for this Property for the duration of the agreement. Applicant agrees the FINANCING SUCCESS FEE is earned on acceptance of commitment and is payable at closing of any loan made on this property during the duration of this agreement.

APPLICANT RESPONSIBILITIES

Applicant agrees to provide the information required by Coast Investors to create the loan request package. Applicant agrees to review the completed loan request package and is responsible for its accuracy. After the loan application has been obtained, Applicant agrees to use due diligence to close the loan. Applicant is responsible to ensure FINANCING SUCCESS FEE is paid out of escrow/closing.

NO GUARANTEE OF FINANCING SUCCESS

COAST INVESTORS agrees to use reasonable commercial efforts to obtain and close financing for the Property.

COAST INVESTORS does not guarantee that financing can or will be obtained. Applicant agrees that COAST INVESTORS will be liable to Applicant for any losses or damages whatsoever in the event financing is not obtained.

FINANCING SUCCESS FEE

Applicant agrees to pay COAST INVESTORS a FINANCING SUCCESS FEE of 1% of the loan amount (minimum $5,000) payable as follows at closing.

This fee is in addition to any fee paid to the Lender if any. The FINANCING SUCCESS FEE is earned upon written acceptance by Applicant of a loan commitment with any lender during the period of this agreement. The fee is payable on loan closing or if applicant withdraws from the loan commitment.

OTHER FEES

Applicant to pay the customary escrow/closing and other reasonable expenses necessary for the closing of said loan, including without limitation title insurance, attorneys' fees, escrow, notary, tax service, recording, structural/seismic report, environmental audit fees, survey fees, credit reports, commitment and standby fees, if any, and appraisals if required.

PAYMENT FROM CLOSING PROCEEDS

Applicant agrees that BROKER and COAST INVESTORS each has the right to require that payment of the FINANCING SUCCESS FEE be made directly out of the proceeds of the loan and disbursed directly from escrow/closing, and Applicant hereby irrevocably appoints BROKER AND COAST INVESTORS its limited Attorney-in-Fact for the sole purpose of issuing instructions to Escrow/Closing Holder to pay the FINANCING SUCCESS FEE directly to BROKER AND COAST INVESTORS. Applicant further agrees that BROKER AND COAST INVESTORS may use this executed Fee Agreement as a demand in escrow/closing, directing Escrow/Closing Holder to pay and remit the loan fee.

SALE OF PROPERTY

If the Applicant sells the property it may be possible for the new owner (BUYER) to finance the property using this "pre-approved" loan. If 1) Applicant has signed a Loan Application under this contract and 2) sells the property, and 3) BUYER finances this property using the same lender with which the Applicant has signed an application.

Then, Applicant will remain responsible for paying the FINANCING SUCCESS FEE. Applicant will pay Coast Investors the fee within five days of loan closing.

TERMINATION OF AGREEMENT

After 30 days, the APPLICANT, BROKER OR COAST INVESTORS may terminate this agreement with a written Notification of termination delivered to the other parties. Coast

Investors will remove the Applicant's access to the site and will stop Applicant directed work (BROKER AND COAST INVESTORS may, at their own discretion, continue to solicit loan quotes from lenders and present them to Applicant). If Applicant or BROKER terminates the agreement and proceeds to close a loan on the subject property within the Duration of this Agreement with any lender that has been contacted by BROKER OR COAST INVESTORS before BROKER AND COAST INVESTORS received written Notification of Termination, then the FINANCING SUCCESS FEE amount and terms of payment remain in force.

DURATION OF AGREEMENT

This agreement shall be valid for a period of one (1) year from date hereof. Unless cancelled in writing by Applicant at the end of said period, this agreement will automatically be extended for an additional 90 days, at the end of which time it will terminate unless extended in writing by both parties.

GOVERNED BY LAWS OF FLORIDA

This Agreement shall be governed by and construed in accordance with the laws of the State of Florida. If legal action is undertaken to enforce or to declare in effect any provision of this Agreement, that legal action shall be venued in the Superior Court of Florida in and for the County of Contra Costa, and the Court, as part of its judgment, shall award reasonable attorney's fees, interest on amount owed to the maximum allowable rate by law and any other related costs to the prevailing party.

MEDIATION OF DISPUTES

In the event any dispute or controversy arises with respect to the subject matter of this agreement or the transaction contemplated herein (including, but not limited to, the parties' rights with respect to payment of commissions as provided herein) which the parties are unable to resolve among themselves after a good faith effort to do so, at the request of either party, All parties to this agreement agree to attempt to resolve such dispute or controversy through mediation in San Francisco pursuant to a mediation conducted by a mediator appointed by the American Arbitration Association in accordance with its mediation rules.

ARBITRATION OF DISPUTES

In the event any dispute or controversy arises with respect to the subject matter of this agreement or the transaction contemplated herein (including, but not limited to, the parties' rights with respect to payment of commissions as provided herein) that is not resolved as provided in paragraph MEDIATION OF DISPUTES Above, Applicant and Coast Investors agree that such dispute or controversy shall be settled by final, binding arbitration in accordance with the Commercial Arbitration Rules of the American Arbitration Association, and judgment upon the award rendered by the arbitrator(s) may be entered in any court that has jurisdiction thereof.

COAST INVESTORS CONTACT INFORMATION

Address: Coast Investors, Inc

BROKER CONTACT INFORMATION

1234 Main Street, Suite 432

Palmetto Bay, FL 33158

786-555-6666

APPLICANT CONTACT INFORMATION

Applicant Name ————————————————————————————

Applicant Address ————————————————————————————

Applicant Phone ————————————————————————————

Applicant Fax ————————————————————————————

Applicant Email ————————————————————————————

APPROVALS

FULL AUTHORITY TO EXECUTE THIS AGREEMENT ON BEHALF OF ALL PARTIES IN INTEREST IS WARRANTED TO BE HELD BY THE UNDERSIGNED.

AGREED TO FOR APPLICANT BY:

——

Authorized Signer for Applicant

——

ACCEPTED AND AGREED TO FOR COAST INVESTORS BY:

——

Authorized Signer for COAST INVESTORS

——

Appendix B: Marketing Letters

Sample Letter: Property Owner

January 1, 2004

Mr. Bertran DuPuy

Coast Investors Properties

007 Ocean Drive.

Miami Beach, FL 33139

Dear Bert:

If you have tried to get a loan for your commercial property in the past only to find that you wasted thousands of dollars in fees from inaccurate loan quotes, then you are not alone. Many mortgage brokers do not understand the elements of a comprehensive underwriting analysis. In order to provide an accurate loan quote, it is important to understand the key underwriting aspects. More importantly, we have representation agreements with over 85 lenders who provide their lending criteria, and, accordingly, we will have the opportunity to structure the loan so that it best suits your needs, providing you with the most optimal loan structure.

Enclosed is a sample underwriting analysis we perform for all of our commercial clients. Because of the professional analysis we do prior to talking to our lenders, we are able to negotiate the best deal on your behalf.

I will call you next week to discuss how we might earn your business, or you can call me at the number below. We specialize in Office, 5+ unit multifamily apartments, mobile home parks, retail, industrial, healthcare, self-storage, hotel and mixed use properties.

Kind Regards,

Joe Broker

(555) 555-5555

Sample Letter: Realtor

January 1, 2004

Mr. Evald DuPuy

Bond Properties

007 England St.

Los Angeles, CA 90012

Dear James:

Mortgage financing is paramount to any successful real estate transaction. Oftentimes, borrowers are unable to secure optimal mortgage financing, causing transactions to be delayed or even never reach the closing table. From a lender's perspective, understanding the financial risk in a transaction is as important as matching a buyer with a seller. A high percentage of commercial property purchasers rely on local commercial banks that may only provide shorter-term recourse loans. At ABC Mortgage, we provide our clients with honest answers and reliable and prompt service.

Pre-arrange reliable financing quotes on your listings to validate asking prices.

Reduce your buyers' costs by arranging long-term, low-cost debt financing.

Introduce refinance scenarios to property owners—create capital for future property acquisitions.

Enclosed is a sample underwriting analysis our company performs for our commercial real estate clients. We represent numerous commercial mortgage lenders throughout the country. Because we perform a comprehensive analysis prior to engaging lenders, we are able to negotiate the best deal on your client's behalf. We would like the opportunity to work with you.

I will call you next week to discuss how I might earn your business, or you can call me at the number below. Our company specializes in office, 5+ unit multifamily apartments, mobile home parks, retail, industrial, healthcare, self-storage, hotel and mixed use properties.

Kind Regards,

Joe Broker

(555) 555-5555

Sample Letter: Financial Advisor

January 1, 2004

Mr. Evald DuPuy

Bond Properties

007 England St.

Los Angeles, CA 90012

Dear James:

Advising your clients regarding their commercial real estate holdings can be a complicated task. Keeping up to date with underwriting parameters and market driven cap rates can be as time-consuming as staying abreast of the new tax law changes.

Enclosed is a sample underwriting analysis I perform for all of my commercial clients. Because I complete a comprehensive analysis prior to talking to my lenders, I am able to negotiate the best deal on your client's behalf, and would like the opportunity to work with you.

I will call you next week to discuss how I might earn your business, or you can call me at the number below. I specialize in office, 5+ unit multifamily apartments, mobile home parks, retail, industrial, healthcare, self-storage, hotel and mixed use properties.

Kind Regards,

Joe Broker

(555) 555-5555

Sample Advertisement

$10,000 in fees for appraisal, environmental, legal and processing. So why didn't I get a loan on my commercial property?

If you are like most commercial property owners, you may have worked with mortgage brokers in the past that promised you a great rate from a great lender. So you paid all the required fees just to find out that you could not get the rate that you were promised and your loan never closed.

At Coast Investors, we are serious about structuring the best loan for our borrowers, and providing accurate loan quotes. If you need to arrange financing on your commercial real estate, call Coast Investors. We will provide you with a sample loan analysis that illustrates our professionalism and level of understanding of your commercial real estate holdings.

(800) 555 – 5555

Specializing in office, 5+ unit multifamily apartments, industrial, retail, mobile home parks, healthcare, self-storage, hotel and mixed use mortgage

123 Commercial Blvd
Miami Beach Florida

Additional Letters

Property Owner
January 1, 2004
Mr. Evald DuPuy
Bond Properties
007 England St.

Los Angeles, CA 90012

Dear Mr. Bond:

Is your commercial property currently financed with your local bank? Many property owners are unaware that they may be able to obtain more attractive and more suitable financing (e.g., 10- to 15-year, long-term, fixed-rate financing) at a more competitive rate by engaging the services of a commercial mortgage broker. An experienced commercial mortgage broker can also expedite the process by performing a first cut underwriting analysis, which is what a lender requires in order to provide an accurate quote in a timely manner.

At no cost to you, I will perform an analysis of your unique needs based on both financing and underwriting factors:

FINANCING REQUIREMENTS

Requested loan term (and amortization.)

Fixed or variable rate (do you ld the property?)

Awareness of the total costs of the loan (e.g., underwriting, appraisal, engineering, environmental, etc.)

Recourse options (can you realize a tax benefit from structuring a nonrecourse transaction vs. full recourse?)

Can we minimize the financing risk and obtain a better rate and term via cross default, cross-collateralization, or by obtaining release provisions?

UNDERWRITING ANALYSIS

Using industry standard underwriting guidelines, I will determine your property's stabilized net cash flow by reviewing your current rent roll and historical income and expenses.

I will estimate the value of your property based on the stabilized net cash flow prior to an appraisal.

I will determine actual LTV and DSCR from an underwriter's perspective.

I will perform a risk analysis based on lease expiration dates.

This valuable service, for which we normally charge $295, is yours FREE just for an opportunity to work with you in the future.

WHY IS THIS IMPORTANT?

Often, the appearance of a loan request at the time of submission differs from the end result of the final term sheet. This is because cash flows vary for every commercial property, and unless we seek to understand the issues beforehand and demonstrate the underwriting risk prior to underwriting, the lender will have difficulty providing an "accurate" quote. Again, this analysis will be done at no cost to you. With relationships with some of the top commercial mortgage lenders in the country, I am able to deliver fast and accurate loan quotes and ultimately fund your loan.

Sincerely,

Evald DuPuy
Property Owner
January 1, 2004
Mr. Evald DuPuy
Coastal Properties
007 Ocean Drive St.

Miami Beach, FL 33139

Dear James:

Many commercial mortgage loans fail to close simply because a broker did not understand the financing aspects of the property and misrepresented the property to the end lender. Subsequently, the property owner wasted time and money and his loan never funded.

Within 24 hours of my first conversation with you, I will provide you with a thorough underwriting analysis of your commercial property based on income and expenses in order to calculate the stabilized net cash flow and support the value of the property. I perform this analysis in the same manner in which lenders underwrite the financing risk of commercial properties.

As I have access to the top commercial mortgage lenders in the country, I can offer you multiple loan programs at very competitive rates. I would be pleased to meet with you to discuss your property and the available loan programs. Again, all of this is at no cost to you.

Sincerely,

Evald DuPuy

Real Estate Brokers

January 1, 2004

Mr. Harvey Realtor

Real Estate Brokers, Inc.

1007 England St.

Miami, FL 33139

Dear Mr. Realtor:

Many commercial mortgage deals fail to close simply because the proposed financing package was improperly prepared or did not meet the standards of the lender. As a result, appropriate financing could not be obtained and the buyer, the seller and the real estate broker walked away from the transaction.

As a commercial mortgage broker, I am offering to qualify your commercial listings for financing. As a service to you, I will provide you, the seller, and the prospective buyers with a thorough underwriting analysis of the property. My analysis, which includes an analysis of the property's income, expenses, rent roll, and other characteristics, is performed in the same manner in which underwriters determine the financing risk of the property.

With this analysis in hand, you will be able to more accurately manage seller and buyer expectations, and provide your clients with the most competitive financing with the best rate and terms available. I offer this service as a professional courtesy to commercial real estate brokers in the area.

Regards,

Evald DuPuy

Conclusion

The true secret to creating a successful commercial mortgage brokerage business is pure determination. Most people fail just at the moment they are about to succeed. Why? Because they give up. They lack the sincere desire to succeed. As long as you keep trying, you'll never fail.

If you REALLY want to succeed, you will. It's that simple. You can have whatever you want out of life if you're willing to do what it takes to get it.

I am in my sixties. I have been in the corporate finance business for over thirty five years. Like everybody else, I have had my ups and my downs. I have had years where my income was well into the seven figures, and I have had years where my income after all business expenses was a negative number. Through it all, I always go back to a line in a book I read when I was in my very early 20s. The name of the book is *Think and Grow Rich*, one can still find it from time to time. The line is, "If you think you can, you will. If you think you can't, you won't." Do you really understand the true meaning behind that line? Think about it for a minute. If you go through life thinking you can't do something, you never will.

Your attitude is the MOST important factor in determining your success. You MUST think positively and be willing to tackle any obstacle that comes along. The fact is you CAN do whatever you put your mind to. You simply have to believe you can. Always believe in yourself above all else.

Surround yourself with positive people who have already made it or are on their way. Get out there and read all of the information you can get your hands on and start making some real money. It's easier than you think.

About the Author

Evaldo Dupuy was born in Cuba in 1945. His father was an eminent medical doctor, and his mother, a much respected lawyer. In 1961, at age 16, Mr. Dupuy joined the Cuban internal forces fighting the communist dictatorship of Fidel Castro. After the failure of the Bay of Pigs Cuban exile invasion, Mr. Dupuy escaped to the United States, where he finished his high school and college education in the state of Kansas. In the early 1970s, after being employed as department manager for three different hospitals, Mr. Dupuy's entrepreneurial spirit led him to a different venture. Back when cable television was in its infancy—before it was considered cool—Mr. Dupuy was intrigued by its potential. A penniless immigrant with a dream, he started a cable television company from the ground up. He made sales pitches to banks and Wall Street lenders to obtain financing; he climbed telephone poles and laid cable during the day, all the while selling the service door-to-door at night. Mr. Dupuy sold the cable company in 1980, and profited from the value he had built into his company. He began offering his successful money-raising capabilities and contacts to others for a fee. Over the ensuing years, Mr. Dupuy has secured financing for cable companies, cellular telephone companies, power plants, Texas oil producers, office buildings, warehouses, car washes, dry cleaners, restaurants, doctor's offices, and more. Today, his investor and lender contacts are vast, ranging from banks, to hard money lenders, to real estate investment trusts specializing in apartment building loans, to small business lenders, to Wall Street c onduits. Mr. Dupuy's database of lenders and investors can be found for a fee at *www.cresguide.com*.

This book and CD set, along with the resources found at *www.cresguide.com*, will impart—to any person willing to put forth an effort—the ability to make a very comfortable income in an uncrowded field.